Young People, New Theatre

Young People, New Theatre is a 'how-to' book, exploring and explaining the process of collaborating creatively with groups of young people across cultural divides.

Organised into exercises, case studies and specific topics, this book plots a route for those wishing to put this kind of theatre into practice. Born out of the hugely successful *Contacting the World* festival, it is the first practical handbook in this field.

Topics include:

- debating the shared world
- what is collaboration?
- different ways of working
- adapting to specific age-groups and abilities
- post-project evaluations.

Noël Greig has been a theatre practitioner since 1967, working as actor, director and playwright. More than fifty of his plays have been produced and performed both in the UK and overseas, and he teaches in a range of contexts, including schools, colleges and universities, running courses in playwriting, acting and theatre history. He is currently involved in making theatre with and for young people, working with youth groups around the world, and encouraging new writing.

Walking into *Contacting the World* 2006, the atmosphere was electric. Over a hundred young people, from all corners of the world were whooping, dancing and singing together – and that was just in the first moments of meeting each other. The twinning process had allowed the participants to go on an amazing journey: befriending, being inspired by and understanding 'strangers'. And in doing so, learning more about themselves. This book is essential for every individual who works with young people, and for anyone who works in theatre.

Keith Saha, Co-Artistic Director, 20 Stories High, Liverpool

This is a practical, necessary, passionate book. Noel Greig understands how theatre is a collaborative and collective process based on the powerful experiences of individual voices and desires. For over three decades, he has forged work through creative partnerships in specific contexts, producing theatre that has brought urgent, liberating and poetic experiences to diverse audiences. That is what has made his understanding of international projects so full of meaning, relevance and beauty. This book connects us with our abilities to create new ways of understanding our worlds.

Paul Heritage, Professor of Drama, Queen Mary, University of London, International Associate, Young Vic Theatre

As a 'founding father' of *Contacting the World*, Noel Greig has guided this international creative exchange through many phases of growth, experiment and achievement. No-one could be better placed to explore the key ideas behind the project, and to suggest how others can use the techniques developed through *Contacting the World* to inform and inspire their own new theatre collaborations.

John McGrath, Artistic Director, Contact

Young People, New Theatre

A practical guide to an intercultural process

Noël Greig

Routledge
Taylor & Francis Group

LONDON AND NEW YORK

First published 2008 by Routledge
2 Park Square, Milton Park, Abingdon, Oxon OX14 4RN

Simultaneously published in the USA and Canada
by Routledge
270 Madison Ave, New York, NY 10016

Routledge is an imprint of the Taylor & Francis Group, an informa business

Typeset in Janson and Univers by
Florence Production Ltd, Stoodleigh, Devon
Printed and bound in Great Britain by
TJ International Ltd, Padstow, Cornwall

British Library Cataloguing in Publication Data
A catalogue record for this book is available from the British Library

Library of Congress Cataloging in Publication Data
Greig, Noël.
  Young people, new theatre: a practical guide to an intercultural process/
  Noël Greig. *1006381454*
    p. cm.
  Includes index.
  1. Children's theater. 2. Theater and youth. I. Title.
  PN3157.G73 2007
  792.02'26 – dc22   2008000607

ISBN10: 0–415–45250–3 (hbk)
ISBN10: 0–415–45251–1 (pbk)
ISBN10: 0–203–89418–9 (ebk)

ISBN13: 978–0–415–45250–2 (hbk)
ISBN13: 978–0–415–45251–9 (pbk)
ISBN13: 978–0–203–89418–7 (ebk)

For Kully Thiarai

Contents

Illustrations

A colour plate section falls between pages 46 and 47
A black and white plate section falls between pages 136 and 137

Figures

Colour plates

1 Workshop, *Contacting the World* 2002. Photo credit: Matt Squire
2 Workshop, *Contacting the World* 2006. Photo credit: John Cooper
3 Street Performance, *Contacting the World* 2006. Photo credit: Mario Popham
4 Akshen (Malaysia), *Contacting the World* 2002. Photo credit: Matt Squire
5 Performance by Sining Kambayoka Ensemble (The Philippines), *Contacting the World* 2006. Photo credit: John Cooper

Black and white plates

Preface

Several years ago I went to India with my colleague Kully Thiarai, to make contact with theatre groups in Delhi. One of the companies was the Pandies, who are part of a huge theatre movement in India that is committed to making new work that reflects the lives and concerns of people who are often disenfranchised and ignored by the social and political systems – particularly young people. Between us, we developed the notion of linking the Pandies with a company in the UK, one that had similar aims. The idea was for the two companies to collaborate with each other and to develop new pieces of work that would explore the experiences of young people in India and the UK. Returning home, Kully and I spoke to John McGrath – the Artistic Director of Contact Theatre in Manchester – and told him about the idea. He immediately said, 'Yes, let's do it' . . . and then said, 'And let's take it one step further . . . why not involve more than two companies? How about six from the UK and six from other parts of the world?'.

The question then was, what methods could we employ to draw young artists from different cultures together in a collaborative enterprise? I mentioned a project I had been involved in some time before – *Young Voices* – a 'twinning' of two schools in the UK. One was a city school in Nottingham with an ethnically diverse intake, and the other an all-white rural school in Norfolk. The idea was for two classes to collaborate with each other, at long-range, over one school term. Through a series of 'inspirational activities' the children developed themes, characters and possible story lines for a play. With myself, they collaborated on the shape and outcome of the final story. With a designer, they designed and made all their costumes, props and the set. With a musician, they created the music. At the end of the process they had *one play* they had created together and *two different productions* of that same play. They presented the play in their schools, and the following week they travelled to an arts centre at a midway point between Nottingham and Norfolk, where they finally met. Two very different groups of children had become engaged with each other's lives at long range, and had created something together. As one of the teachers said, 'This was not just about the making of a play. It was about the development of young lives'.

John, Kully and I decided that the methodology of *Young Voices* could be adapted to the project we were embarking on: the 'twinning of difference'. The upshot of this was *Contacting the World*, which twinned six partner-groups of young artists, all engaged in the same process, over a nine-month period, and resulted in a festival of new theatre from all over the world. There have now been four *Contacting the World* projects, and the creative work that has developed from them has been taken up and adapted by many other groups and companies who wish to create their own projects. This book is the result of that work. It makes available the ethos, ideas and practical activities that can help inspire the making of new theatre by young people.

Who the book is for

This book is for all groups of young people and young artists – including their older or professional colleagues, teachers, project leaders etc. – who are making new theatre. In particular, it is for groups who wish to engage with the process of 'twinning': the creative collaboration between different groups of young people or artists, with an emphasis on intercultural collaboration.

The practical material in the book can be used and adapted to a broad range of contexts: the school or college drama project, the independent youth theatre group, the professional team of young artists.

How to use the book

The book is arranged into ten chapters. Each chapter has a specific theme or topic.

Chapter 1

The first part of the chapter is an introduction to the idea of twinning. It reflects on a broad theoretical and philosophical context for the work – taking in social, political and cultural aspects of the world we live in, the role of art and the artist, and the creative development of the child and the young person.

The final part of the chapter offers guidance on:

- practical aspects of a twinning project;
- key challenges of such a project;
- what the major aims of such a project might be.

Chapters 2–10

These chapters are of a practical nature, offering a full range of theatre-making activities that can stimulate a twinning project. They are arranged in the following manner:

- *Chapter heading.* A specific activity-area related to the creative process.
- *Activities.* Through-numbered practical work that engages with the chapter heading.
- *Examples.* Work drawn from previous intercultural twinning projects. Some of these examples are quite extensive and take the form of mini 'case studies'. They are, as a resource for the reader, as important as the activities themselves. They add living voices to the practical work and demonstrate the diversity of outcomes that can be inspired by it.
- *Outcomes.* A résumé of where an activity or a chapter has taken the project.
- *Cross-reference.* Between activities, examples and chapters where useful and appropriate.
- *Comment.* From participants of previous intercultural twinning projects. The voices of young artists, groups and companies offer essential advice and critical observation on the process, all of use to the reader as another resource.

Working with the chapters

Although the chapters and activities are arranged in a sequence, the following points of guidance should be taken into account:

- *Selecting your activities.* The activities in the chapters are offered as a broad and comprehensive range of work related to the chapter heading. It will be up to each project to choose the ones that inspire them most, or that are most appropriate to the nature and context of the project.
- *Pick and mix.* The making of a piece of theatre does not happen as schematically as the chapters are laid out. As your project develops, you may well need to go back and forth between chapters. Treat the chapters not as a rigid 'set menu', but more of a buffet or a picnic – dip in and out of the chapters as appropriate to your needs.
- *Inspire yourself.* All of the work in the book is intended to be an 'inspirational guide' as opposed to a 'mechanistic formula'. If you find that activities of your own devising are being inspired, then trust them and go with them. Return to the book later if you feel you are going 'off course'. If the book really *is* working for you, then there will be times when you can set it aside. Hopefully the book will prove a good and trusted 'leader' for you – but leaders should never be indispensable!

Acknowledgements

This book could not have been written without the work, energy, enthusiasm, intelligence and sheer joy of life and creativity of all the young people and young artists (and their older colleagues and collaborators) I have encountered through twinning projects. The bulk of the practical work derives from the context of the *Contacting the World* projects, which – by the time the book goes to print – will have engaged with forty-eight groups from around the world and many hundreds of participants. Other projects – no less significant, even if smaller in scale and scope – have enabled the inclusion of further work. The major thanks for inspiring this book go to all those people.

I would like to thank in particular all those individuals who have given up their time to help me gather together all the source material for the book: young people and young artists, group leaders and teachers, project managers and artistic facilitators. I sincerely apologise in advance if I have failed to mention anyone from the huge cast of people who have assisted me in my task.

Segun Adelfila, Eliane Adorno, Adel Al-Salloum, Shabina Aslam, Ananda Breed, Alwyn Walsh, Jimmy David, Hanne M. de Bruin-Rajagopal, Zac Dodoo, Tearlach Duncasson, Thierry Gomes, Felipe Gonzalves, Paul Heritage, Omoaluse Igberaese, Paul James, Michael Judge, Sanjay Kumar, Dbora Landim, John McGrath, Hettie Malcolmson, Jamile Menezes, Borhan Mohammadi, Kelly Morgan, Yinka Ola-Williams, Victor Porfirio, Alan Richardson, Joao Andre da Rocha, Julia Samuels, Joao Santana, Fabio Santos, Sam Scott, Simon Sharkey, Amit Sharma, Claudia Spencer, Martin Stannage, Brian Talbi, Diane Thornton, Julia Turpin, Neil Verani, Julie Ward, Sunny Wray, Rachel Yates, Madani Younis.

1 The twinning process

Never doubt that a small group of thoughtful, committed people can change the world. Indeed, it's the only thing that ever has.

(Margaret Mead)

You can't transform the whole world, but a small group can go very far in transforming at all levels relationships within itself, and with its immediate audience during a performance.

(Peter Brook)

Making theatre is to enter into an unknown world, to enter on a stage of liberation.

(A nine-year-old pupil in Brazil)

This book is primarily a practical guide to a specific process of creative work: the twinning of groups of young artists from different cultures and communities, leading to new theatre that is rooted in a collaborative enterprise. The work it offers is based upon proven methods, examples and outcomes of creative activities, all of which can be adopted and adapted to a range of contexts.

This work has not come out of thin air. The projects that inspired the work in this book – ones that I have been personally involved with – were themselves inspired by a movement and developments in new theatre that have been evolving for some time; a youth theatre movement that exists outside or alongside the institutional structures; groups of young people making theatre that is not part of an overly formal, educationally driven structure, with working practices and outcomes that are not too 'programmatic'; new theatre developments, initiated and driven by young artists entering the professional field, that challenge the ways in which theatre is made and what its purpose and function are. This book comes out of that history.

It also comes out of a broader history – the re-evaluation of the role of creativity and artistic processes in an evolving world. That is, 'art' not just as an add-on to 'real life' (a leisure pursuit to be consumed after the daily battle with material circumstances) – nor indeed as a mechanistic 'solution' to particular social or economic problems. The re-evaluation I refer to addresses the major question of our times: 'How do we release our human creativity in ways that may steer us, in a truly evolutionary way, from the seemingly self-destructive path we have set ourselves on?'.

That question is, of course, a tall order for a book that has a specific brief: the exploration of a particular theatre process. It would be grandiose of me to suggest that I'll be answering the question in its totality. But I would like you to view the work offered as one aspect of a worldwide movement in the arts – one that is 'under the radar' of the cultural mandarins and policymakers, but that may just signal some new way forward.

I would like you to see the work – and your own creative projects – in this context. Therefore, this opening chapter begins with a broad theoretical, political and philosophical reflection on some of the thinking that has inspired it. In all the things I will be referring to – history, cultural developments, neurobiology, globalisation and economics – I am no 'expert'. But they are all things that artists are interested in and that increasingly – particularly among young artists – form part of our reflection on the purposes of creative activity in our shared world.

Nor are artists alone in their consideration of the place of art in the world. There is a gradual, often fragmentary, but observable shift in the perception of creative collaboration taking place within other areas of thought and action. I was recently at a gathering of scientists and artists. It is an ongoing forum and it is called the Tipping Point. The 'tipping point' is an image related to a mechanism such as the water-wheel: the point at which the cumulative pressure of a process – slow and undetectable at first – builds to the moment when there is a massive and unstoppable rate of change. The forum was concerned with climate change and was styled as 'a continuing dialogue between artists and people engaged in researching and understanding climate change'. The purpose of the forum was not to 'listen to experts', but to engage the two disciplines in a creative dialogue around 'how to respond to this new and extraordinary challenge'. What was extraordinary for me – as someone who became a practising theatre artist in the 1960s – was to hear a major climate-change scientist say that 'we need artists, now more than ever, to work with and collaborate with'. I say 'extraordinary' because, when I began my work, the notion of scientists regarding artists as equal partners would have sounded like pie in the sky. Yet here at this gathering were major figures from the world of science saying that artists could – and must – be collaborators with them in reimagining the world.

The creative collaborations between young people – groups of professional artists or youth theatre groups – that have inspired this book are firmly within the context of all the above remarks. That is: making new theatre that is appropriate for the time we live in.

Towards the end of the chapter there will be guidance and comment on practical aspects of the twinning process, key challenges of such projects, and possible aims. For those readers who wish to engage immediately with such matters, please do not hesitate to turn to them first. But I would suggest that you find time to come back to the opening section of the chapter when you feel that may be appropriate or useful.

TWINNING IN A GLOBAL CONTEXT

The following thoughts, reflections and comments represent – in a distilled form – the wide-ranging dialogues between artists I have collaborated with: many of them young practitioners and others (such as myself) a bit longer in the tooth. All have been focussed on the *new context* for the artist in the world. All of them draw upon a keen perception of the forces that are operating in the world and how they affect our lives and futures.

A world in transit

In the eighteen months between my starting to write this book and its publication, huge numbers – possibly millions – of people around the world will have experienced major shifts in their lives: geographical, social, cultural and economic. The conditions of life (in all its aspects) will have changed fundamentally, often without much prior warning and without the benefit of traditional survival codes. These changes will have required the need to adapt, often swiftly and brutally. In the newspaper today, for instance, I read of a scheme that involves the demolition and compulsory eviction of tens of thousands of slum-dwellers in the Dharavi district of Mumbai. The district is a prime property-development site, and the 60,000 families will be shifted in order to make way for expensive residential apartments, new office buildings and an industrial park. Putting aside the fact that the residents of Dharavi have been promised 'brand new homes' (the word 'promised' is key here), it is worth noting that Mumbai's government has declared that the scheme will not require the usual seventy per cent approval of the local inhabitants. The compulsory razing of Dharavi and the displacement of its people will have taken place without their consent. The change will have been imposed 'from the top'.

'Change' has of course always been a constant factor in human history. Human beings have always been 'on the move'. Mass migrations, shifts in populations, wars, slavery, colonialism, famines and the effects (and possible benefits) of developing technologies have all contributed to the transformation of the securities and certainties of 'the traditional' and 'the known' into the challenges of 'the new'.

However, it is safe to say that such processes are now happening at unprecedented levels and on a scale and at a pace never known before. The example of Dharavi in Mumbai is just one of the countless mega-schemes that we read or hear about daily. On smaller scales too, the collusion of big business and local and national governments imposes changes that disrupt the fabric of life. In England, a small village will disappear under the tarmac of a new airport runway; a row of perfectly good houses is demolished to make way for a motorway bypass. The experience of change (in all its dimensions) is becoming *the* determinant factor of life for everyone, and the insecurities, fears – and possibly the occasional exhilaration – that change can bring are heightened by the rapidity with which it occurs.

Even when we are not personally or immediately affected by certain aspects of change, the very fact that we are aware of them can add to the sense of apprehension that comes of living in 'a world in transit'. The place of safety (tradition, belief, culture or community) seems to disappear in the face of the unknown 'new' that lurks around the corner. The technological media beam into our very homes the images of the great transitions taking place. We see the migrations into great new cities of people from previously rural, agricultural economies. We are aware of the destruction of old and stable – if often poverty-ridden – ways of life, through rapid industrialisation, natural disaster (often aided by human ineptitude and greed), mass tourism etc. We know that countless people make desperate journeys across dangerous seas on insubstantial craft or in sealed trucks, to seek a better life on other continents. Governments woo workers from other lands to come and do low-paid and unsafe work. Political asylum seekers seek refuge from cruel and tyrannical regimes. And politicians and 'leaders' (with a few honourable exceptions) grab onto the statistics and play on our anxieties to gain votes or hang on to power: 'our way of life' is being threatened, we are 'being swamped' by 'alien' cultures, our 'cultural heritage' and our fundamental beliefs are 'under siege'. And so – whether or not we are personally threatened – we perceive the world as a place that is shifting, dangerous and out of our control. And, unfortunately, we have the tendency to place the blame for this on the very people who are 'swamping' us, who are 'alien', who are 'threatening our jobs'. This is perhaps the greatest danger we face – the impulse to fear 'the other', to close ranks and to reject anything and anyone who is different. For we are living at a moment in history when – like it or not – we need to adapt to existing cheek by jowl with each other in ways that have never occurred before.

This is the world that young people are coming into and having to deal with. It is – if we simply go by the things just mentioned – a pretty gloomy prospect. So it is worthwhile remembering that 'in transit' can also bring benefits and opportunities – equally challenging, but with some promise of good outcomes. The benefits of cheap travel (the question of 'the carbon footprint' aside, for the moment) have meant that students have been able to experience life and learning in different countries and cultures. Some forms of travel (the ones that do not simply drop us down into expensive resorts in exotic places) have opened eyes, ears, hearts and minds to the possibility that 'the other' is not so *very* different to us. The arrival and presence of people from another culture in 'our' community are not always and inevitably shaped by the fears vote-seeking politicians attempt to instill in us. I am reminded of a rural community in England recently, in which an African family had settled. Such communities can often be a little inward-looking and suspicious of 'the outsider', but in this case, when the Home Office attempted to repatriate the family to its country of origin, the community rallied round and fought off the government. The family stayed. A tiny example, certainly, in which the experience of 'a world in transit' does not result in fear and suspicion of 'the stranger' – but there will be countless others, even if the 'official' picture gives them little recognition.

The challenge of change

Nevertheless, it would be foolish not to recognise that an aspect of human nature is a sort of innate conservatism: a desire for the safety and security of 'the known', and a predisposition to suspicion and fear of 'the new'. Even when – through necessity, coercion or a sense of adventure – we venture into a new environment, we have an impulse to carry with us, or recreate, the symbols of our known and secure worlds. Nineteenth-century European 'explorers' into Africa took with them the trappings of their bourgeois world. 'Native' muscle and sweat dragged European implements, furnishings and bedding across deserts and through forests. In more modern times, the package-holiday trade from northern to southern Europe has seen the arrival of the 'English pub' in the resorts of Spain and Portugal, catering for the need to 'be abroad' and 'be at home' at the same time. A friend of mine, whose family moved to the UK from rural India, tells me how her mother reproduced in full detail her Asian village environment in an English terrace house kitchen – the implements, decorations, foodstuffs, language and total *feel* of the place.

This need to *replicate the known* (and keep the strange at bay) seems to be an imperative that exists in all cultures. Such strategies are clearly designed to lessen the aggravation, confusion, apprehensions and tensions of the con-tact zones between different cultures and environments. But these protective devices, harmlessly conservative as they may seem, can mask an underlying aggression towards 'the other' – a resistance to absorbing the new and the 'alien'. We can be critical of this and take a moral or political stance – the image of the feather-bedded nineteenth-century European being carried around Africa by native bearers is as dubious as the notion of the English pub being deposited in the middle of a twentieth-century Spanish village. The attempt of an Asian woman to reproduce her home village in an English terrace house seems equally defensive, even if possibly more understandable in the face of entering a dominant environment that is hostile to her presence in the first place.

All of the above examples of this tendency to want to carry our known culture with us, like the turtle with her shell, are relatively harmless on a global scale. None of them suggests a major threat to human evolution or the end of the species. Yet all of them suggest that there might be something amiss in our resistance to the new, and particularly when we look at this tendency in terms of our rapidly changing world. Looking at the big, global issues that face us, this failure to embrace the new begins to take on more alarming dimensions. The current rise of certain forms of fundamentalism, the possibility of a new arms race, the reappearance of vigorous forms of nationalism all suggest that we have evolved our protective shields to the point where our capacity for mutual distrust has led us into the dangerous territory of mutual destruction. The question arises: Has our 'innate conservatism' (survival, a sense of identity) outlived its usefulness? Or is it our destiny?

Do we have the capacity to think about this and – through thinking – discover new and creative ways to avoid the 'tipping point'? Recent research into the human brain and its development may offer some optimism here.

The human brain

Scientific research into the human brain and its development suggests that innate conservatism and its negative or destructive outcomes are not our destiny. For those of us who are interested in developing strategies – in the arts or otherwise – for tackling the challenge of change that faces the world, this work sheds helpful light upon our task.

Recent developments in the field of neurobiology have revealed that this 'innate conservatism' exists in the structures of the brain and how it develops. That is, there is a *scientific basis* for our resistance to change. Without going into this in huge detail, the research has shown some of the following.

In early age (childhood), the human brain – in its developing structure – is remarkably 'plastic' in its ability to absorb and be literally shaped by its environment. For example, the ability to absorb – and adapt – that is observed in the child's brain is shown in the greater ease with which children learn new languages compared with adults. Another – and truly distressing – example of the ability of the child to absorb and adapt to the influences of new information can be found in some accounts of the concentration camps during the Nazi regime in Germany. Here, there were reports of children's games called 'going to the gas chamber'.

By early adulthood, however, the brain has become much less 'plastic' – the elaborate structures developed in childhood begin to show a *diminished ability to change*. A sort of 'hardening of the adaptive arteries' is an image that comes to mind. From being the 'absorbing–adapting' structure of the 'child brain', it becomes an organ (the adult 'mind') whose structures are established. The previous, more receptive, activity of the brain changes to that of 'going out'. It now seeks to make the world around it (environment etc.) conform to its established structures. This process – according to the research into neurobiology – begins in early adulthood. Our need to 'shape the world' is therefore based on the imperative of the brain to ensure that the *external* structures of the world – the whole environment – match its *internal* structures.

The above is putting into a very small nutshell a massive amount of research into the physical development of the brain and its structures. To go into it in any further detail is beyond the remit of this book, but, even if we consider this abbreviated account, it casts a new light on our behaviour as human beings – how we interact with each other as individuals and groups, socially, culturally and historically. Suddenly, the difficulties facing groups or individuals when their 'known' environment changes – through immigration, imprisonment, exile, migration, the destruction of a settled habitat, the development of new technologies etc. – are understood in a new way. In such circumstances, the 'external' (the symbolic environment) no longer matches with the 'internal' (the structured brain). The discomfort and trauma this can produce – personal, inter-group, inter-ethnic etc. – can be immense. But now that trauma can be viewed not just as some eternal, unsolvable or feckless aspect of human nature, to be 'solved' by war, conquest or martial law (or by being nice to the maids and the waiters in our 'exotic holiday retreat'!). It is rooted in the codes laid down in the brain. The struggle to 'control the story' – to demand consistency between internal structure and external reality – is lodged in our evolution.

So what does all this mean to us, living in this world 'in transit', where the contact zones between different cultures, faiths, beliefs, traditions and ways of life multiply daily? What strategies are available or possible for minimising the actual or perceived threats that turn these meeting places into battlefields? For find them we must, if we do not wish the defensive, structured and 'non-plastic' brain (mind) to overwhelm us in fundamentalist ways of thinking and behaving, increased state controls, more 'gated communities', 'exclusion walls' and border controls.

Once again, all this seems a recipe for gloom and doom. Are we condemned (in Greek tragedy style) by the very nature of our neurobiology to a repetition of cycles of mutual distrust and destruction that become even more regular and overwhelming? It is not the place of this book to provide the answer or the solution. But – in the particular field of human activity it deals with, and within the specific scope of what it offers – it does provide one strategy for dealing with the challenge of change. And that is based upon the ways in which human creativity – through the arts and the collaborative processes they offer – can provide what the politicians and war lords and multinational corporations have failed to provide. Which is the opportunity to turn the contact zone between different cultures into a creative interface, as opposed to a war zone. Not necessarily a 'place of harmony', where there is a watering-down of everything (that dreadful, sentimental 70s pop song that said all the world needs is a 'great big melting-pot'), but a place where a genuine fusion of cultures creates 'the new' without wiping out the best of 'the old'.

Change and its symbols

For those of us working in the arts – particularly where new forms of art are developing at cultural interfaces – the research into neurobiology provides us with specific evidence not only of *the problems* but also of *the opportunities* that the challenge of change presents.

If *resistance to change* is rooted in the structures of the non-plastic brain (mind) that appear in early adulthood, then that is part of our *evolutionary development*: the need of the human to survive and to feel safe – to control the environment. The development of symbols – signifiers of the group identity – was key to that imperative. The development of a brain (mind) that demanded and made external symbols to match its own structures was necessary in a world where food, shelter and safety were the pressing needs. Where the competition for these (perhaps not the least from other species as well as other groups of humans or pre-humans) was fierce, the human need to control and adapt the environment to the needs of the group came to the fore, as did the symbol-creating capacity.

Food, shelter and safety are of course still the pressing needs. Now, however, we know that, if we wished to organise ourselves decently, all could be provided without conflict. Unfortunately, the ideologies and symbols we have created – and the systems we have set in place that reflect them – seem rooted in our non-plastic brain (mind): the urge to control, dominate and compete. Think of national flags, monuments and statues; hammers and sickles, swastikas and royal regalia; sky-scrapers, superjets and Olympic stadiums. The symbols of our world spell out 'competition is all'.

This is not to say that an element of competition may not have its place in a healthy spectrum of human behaviours. There is no harm, I believe, in delighting in 'our team winning'. Or coming first in the egg-and-spoon race at the school sports day (though some silly people have tried to ban such things, as being too 'physically risky'). Or getting the best exam results (though some silly people have tried to abolish the notion that one never 'fails' an exam). But any culture or society in which 'competition' becomes the predominant factor in the *management* of the world is clearly unhealthy in the extreme. Which is where we seem to have got ourselves. The usefulness of the non-plastic (territorial, controlling, non-absorbing) brain seems to have outstripped its usefulness entirely. Our symbolic and technological control and depiction of the world seem to threaten our survival: the tipping point where our addiction to the redundant symbols of the past means that we'll have non-evolved ourselves out of existence.

There is a joke – or trick question – I heard once. Question: 'What is the link between Neanderthal Man and fully developed human beings?' Answer: 'Us.'

We need to change our symbols if we are to evolve – and this is where the artist can be of the greatest use.

The evolutionary artist

So, at this juncture in our short but literally explosive occupation of the planet, are we still capable of evolving, and in a manner that is creative rather than destructive? Are there strategies that our very clever – but not always overly intelligent – brains can develop to aid this evolution? Strategies that, at the moment, do not take centre-stage alongside the sabre-rattling of politicians and the wheeler-dealing of the multinational corporations? How can we participate in our own evolution?

This book – all the practical work it contains and the projects that the work has come from – is firmly based on the understanding that *participation in creative-arts activity* is much, much more than a pleasant pastime. The practical work it offers – and the outcomes of that work for the many people from a huge range of cultures and communities – is evidence that such activity can affect change in ways that laws, regulations, wars, invasions or ideological positions can never do. By this I mean *evolutionary change* in the ways that our brains (minds) develop, and consequently how we see ourselves, how we see each other, and how we interact.

To suggest – in the face of all the evidence around us of a world in crisis – that 'the artist' and 'artistic creativity' can play a crucial part in the evolution of our species seems almost laughable. In the hard-nosed world of politics, economics and military tactics, the notion that 'art' (or the participation in artistic creation) has any part to play in effecting real 'change' is not on the agenda. Where they are taken 'seriously' (in the culture I live in, at least), 'the arts' do gain some credibility when they can be mechanistically 'justified' in some way or another. By contributing to the national balance of payments (tourism), by adding to state prestige (cultural dominance), by alleviating the worst aspects of an unfair state (social engineering), or by providing a diversion from 'real life' (bread and circuses). Some of these things are not necessarily bad in themselves, but – and here is a great paradox – *art* is given a role or a function, but the notion of *the artist* is still derided. Or feared.

Why is the artist feared?

The fear of the artist

I return to the research into the brain as it has evolved so far and the findings that research into neurobiology has revealed.

The process of 'growing up' seems to be culturally linked to a rejection (or dismissal) of the early-age, absorbing, adapting and receptive activity of the brain in favour of the environment-shaping activity that replaces it from early adulthood. Again, I can only speak with full confidence from the direct – and therefore subjective – experience of my own culture (Western European and Christian-based), where 'childhood' is regarded as a sort of chaotic pre-cursor to full human status. However, my contact with other cultures, through my work, has indicated that the dismissal of the child – her perceptions, insights, abilities etc. – is found everywhere in varying degrees (not the least in most state educational structures). And it is fascinating to note the similarity of terms by which 'the child' and 'the artist' are referred to. Terms such as 'naïve', 'innocent', 'unworldly', 'incomprehensible', 'muddled', 'unruly', 'chaotic', 'un-disciplined' come to mind. All these, of course, are paradoxically set against the representation of certain artists or children as 'gifted', 'the genius', 'the visionary', 'the prodigy' etc. But all of them – the dismissive, the derogatory and the worshipful – place both the child and the artist somehow outside of 'the normal'. And in all cases there is the implication that there is something here to be wary of – to be controlled or harnessed, either by being disciplined or put on a pedestal. The need to control something springs from a fear of that thing. A rising crime rate, a rebellious underclass, a forbidden sexual desire, the unruly child . . . or the artist whose perception of the world unsettles, challenges and subverts the *symbols* that the non-plastic brain (mind) requires for its sense of security.

The history of the repression (fear) of the artist, in all cultures, as a sub-versive is well recorded. In England, during the Puritan revolution of the seventeenth century, the theatres were closed. In the eighteenth century, the English colonisers of Ireland outlawed the teaching of the native language (its stories and culture), giving rise to the resistance movement of the 'hedgerow teachers', who (under pain of death) kept the culture alive by pass-ing on the stories and tales in secret. The fascist and state-communist regimes of the twentieth century gave rise to hysterical and deadly responses to new forms of art. In Nazi Germany the diatribe against jazz music combined a fear of spontaneity with outright racism – 'jungle music' being of course the product of lesser ('infantile') black races. In Stalin's Russia, new forms of theatre, music and painting were regarded as the bourgeois pollutants of 'pure' proletarian art. Major theatre artists such as Meyerhold were murdered or sent to the Gulags. In China, under the Cultural Revolution of Mao, all forms of theatre that did not depict the state ideology were banned, and artists were murdered. In the USA, during the 1950s' anti-communist witch hunts, playwrights and other artists whose work was regarded as 'un-American' were silenced. British Empire apologists still fondly believe it spread freedom of thought (a myth that US neo-cons have adopted for themselves recently with regard to the Middle East). But a recent exhibition displayed the vast amount of material – plays, novels, poems, histories, films – that the British made sure that their Indian subjects would not have access to. The representation of the human body through art has been, and is still is, an ideological battleground. In the USA, public galleries were forced to withdraw the work of photog-rapher R. Mapplethorpe – the naked male body was too much for 'decent folk'. In Afghanistan, the Taliban destroyed ancient cultural religious symbols that did not fit with their view of the world as it should be perceived and organised, and music and dancing were banned. In Turkey, novelists are murdered and imprisoned by the state. Recently, in Germany, the archbishop of Cologne has called some modern art 'degenerate' – a chilling throwback to the same word that the Nazis used for modern (often Jewish) art and music. In India, in 1989, Safdar Hashmi was murdered while his theatre group, Jana Natya Manch, was staging a street play in support of wage increases for industrial workers. As I write, news has just come in from Uzbekistan of the murder of Mark Weil, a theatre director whose theatre company Ilkhom challenged political repression in that country. '*Ilkhom*' means 'inspiration' in Uzbek.

Even where outright banning, imprisonment and murder are not on the agenda, other ways of containing and controlling artists are manifold. There is co-option into 'the establishment'. In the UK, previously republican play-wrights bow to the monarch and accept a knighthood. There is the 'defence of the traditional'. The (often genuine) fears and anxieties that a global world, dominated by American-style culture, will wipe out distinct cultural art forms have seen governments attempt to enforce and preserve 'the traditional', but at a cost – usually resulting in authentic art forms becoming another dead spectacle for tourists to gape at. There are the 'gatekeepers of culture' in the so-called liberal societies. Critics, academics, pundits etc. use the channels of the media to present their tastes and preferences as the accepted view of what is 'good art' and 'bad art'. There are dangerous liaisons with private or business sponsorships. A national theatre company in the UK was refused much-needed corporate sponsorship for its production of a Jacobean tragedy, '*Tis Pity She's A Whore*, because the corporation did not wish its name to be associated with the word 'whore'. A private art collector buys up – at huge expense – the early work of new, young and potentially subversive fine artists, turning both art and artist into 'brands'. These are the subtle enchantments of commerce and the fees it pays. A radical 60s 'beat poet' lends his image to the glossy selling of a brand of leisure wear in the 90s.

All states, all ideologies, all attempts to impose a world-view and a form of society have their strategies for controlling art and its production. The tools may be different, but the aim is the same. The sponge of capitalism soaks up dissenting art, markets it and sells it back for a profit. The hammer of communism or fascism smashes the bones of artists. The silken veil of liberalism is drawn across that which it does not wish us to see.

The front-line artist

None of this works in the end, of course, even though many artists have been killed, silenced, sidelined, bought off or co-opted in the meantime. I have already mentioned the 'hedgerow teachers' in Ireland in the eighteenth century. There is always resistance. Art – the human need to create – will just not go away. Beneath the evolutionary need of the structured, non-plastic brain to control the symbols of the world lies that other thing: the creative, absorbing and adaptive brain – of 'the child', of 'the artist'. And it continues to make itself heard with resilience and continued renewal.

Much of this happens 'in the margins', and it would be foolish to claim that the plastic brain structures of the pre-adult mind will be the basis of a new evolutionary drive that saves us from ourselves. But it might just be that – midway between the somewhat hazy hope of a 'spiritual renewal' and the possibly arrogant belief in 'technological progress' – the next phase in our human evolution lies within the neuropsychological structures of the brain. That the dead-end we seem to have reached may turn us back to find another path – one that reimagines the world, its symbols and the ways we work together. The artistic gifts within all of us – repressed as they might be – may be the evidence of the possibility of such an evolution.

On a practical, observable level there are some optimistic signs that the artist and artistic creativity may not be quite so 'on the margins' as we are led to believe. I return to the Tipping Point – the front line debate between scientists and artists on how the two disciplines may collaborate on the issue of global warming. After the two days I spent in Oxford at a recent Tipping Point event, several people said to me, when I told them about it, 'But how can art have anything to do with solving the problem?'. I think that is the wrong question. Art cannot 'solve' anything, and the moment it attempts to do so it stops being art and abandons itself to the agendas of the social engineers. As Oscar Wilde said:

> whenever a community or a powerful section of society of a community, or a government of any kind, attempts to dictate to the artist what he is to do, art either vanishes, or becomes stereotyped, or degenerates into a low and ignoble form of craft.
>
> (Oscar Wilde, *The Soul of Man under Socialism*)

The question should perhaps be Oscar Wilde's own: 'What is a healthy or an unhealthy work of art?' Oscar, in talking about the artist, was primarily concerned with the individual artist: 'a healthy work of art is one the choice of whose subject is conditioned by the temperament of the artist, and comes directly out of it'. But – as he was a socialist (he was despised as much for this as he was for his homosexuality) – I think that he may have appreciated the type of collaborative artistic work this book is concerned with. And as such, his notion of what is an unhealthy work of art applies in both instances:

> An unhealthy work of art . . . is a work whose style is obvious old fashioned and common, and whose subject is deliberately chosen, not because the artist has any pleasure in it, but because he thinks that the public will pay him for it.
>
> (Oscar Wilde, *The Soul of Man under Socialism*)

For Oscar, art should be a 'disturbing and disintegrating force'. That is, something that is on the front line of challenging the easy, lazy, corrupt and conformative ways in which the world is perceived, organised and *symbolised*.

So, if we talk of an alliance of artists and scientists around the issue of global warming, the 'healthy' work of the artist will not be to become a mere mouthpiece for statistics and strategies. It will be about a passionate pleasure in creating new symbols and stories that jolt us out of the lazy complacency that seems to be leading us, like sleepwalkers, into the abyss. 'But *how?*' some people asked when I had come back from the Tipping Point event.

Well, if we want examples of how art *can* create new symbols and stories that are appropriate for the time, we could look at Picasso's *Guernica*. This representation of war and the shadow of fascism about to overwhelm Europe did not stop either of these – but the disturbingly new visualisation of both offered the opportunity to *think* about both in different ways. We could also look at the response of artists worldwide to the AIDS epidemic and the lies, slanders and silences that surround it. Again, artistic work has not stopped HIV/AIDS, but it has created symbols and stories that have shifted the *perceptions* about it in ways that the heroic work of the scientific and medical worlds could never do. Plays, novels, film, photography, music, dance, poetry, paintings – all have contributed to a huge shift in the ways in which AIDS is perceived.

Art, by allying itself to the great issues of the day, need not be the 'unhealthy' conformist art that Oscar despised. Indeed, through its ability to disturb and disrupt, it can transform our perceptions of the world more effectively than any government-inspired strategy can ever do. And the continuing challenge for all artists is the question, 'Are we moral agents or the servants of power?'.

All this may seem to have taken me a long way from the focus of this book: the twinning of young artists from different cultures in collaborative creative work. But – if we are talking about artists being on the 'front line' of change – then it is young artists who must lead the troops. It is 2007 and I am 62. Some of the young artists I work with are 18. In 2050 they will be 61. I will be long gone, and the world will have changed immeasurably. The gloomy predictions may have won the day, but I have a hunch that we may be in for some surprises of the optimistic kind – if we nurture the soil they may grow from. And that is by investing in the creative wisdom and energies of young people.

The work offered in this book is seemingly small and insignificant in the face of the challenges of the world we share. But if we see it in a larger context – one thread in a tapestry that is being woven worldwide – it begins to enlarge. The work the book may inspire could be small-scale and local, or larger-scale and international. But if it encourages 'the creative new', through a process of collaboration and mutual respect, not competition, conquest and mutual distrust, then it will have contributed to the making of new symbols to guide our evolution.

Some years ago I worked with a group of young people on a playwrighting project. One young woman – age about 16 – came up with a phrase during one exercise that has always stayed with me. Her words caught the essence of how an artist can represent the world in a way that is symbolic, complex, disturbing and 'true'. It combines the individual, the collective, the particular and the universal. It is one of the most beautiful – and useful – pieces of word-symbolism I have ever encountered, and it continues to inspire me:

In this universe we all play a different tune on the same violin.

FAMILIAR USES OF TWINNING

Although the work in this book is concerned with a particular form of twinning groups of people in a creative process, 'twinning' is something that has become a familiar strategy in certain cultural and educational enterprises. It is useful to see our work in this broader context.

Twinning as a process of interaction between towns from different countries is something that has been developed in different ways over recent years. It has enabled groups of residents to share and exchange activities, interests and histories. As such, this type of interaction between cultures replaces the rather arid notion of 'tourism' with an active engagement between people – a 'twinned regatta' or exchange visits by amateur orchestras are infinitely more creative than trooping round monuments with cameras at the ready.

In the educational field, twinning has also been adopted as a strategy for broadening the experience of the pupils. Schools with significantly different ethnic intakes have worked together, thus breaking down barriers between a town's ethnic communities. Activities have ranged from the specifically religious – visits to mosques and churches – to joint drama, art and music projects. Schools have held shared assemblies, and children have been encouraged to write to pupils at other schools by email. Such work has also taken on an international dimension, encouraging pupils to develop a global standpoint and equip them for a world that is in transit – an interconnected world where, in the future, more people will work overseas, and one in four jobs will be related to international trade. International partnerships between schools can involve a single project, or can be about developing a three-year programme. Cultural visits, a diverse range of language teaching, staff exchanges and online collaborations are part of the range of opportunities on offer. International work can be woven across the curriculum, rather than confined to one or two subject areas. All this can uproot budding prejudices and deepen the pupil's knowledge of how the world works. The fostering of the notion of 'the global citizen' and a common humanity that can develop from such activities is – at their best – an invaluable tool for facing the challenges of a rapidly changing world. A major European project has brought together thousands of schools from twenty-eight countries, stretching from Iceland to the Balkans, each 'twinning' developing its own 'learning area'. A school in England forged links with a school in Ghana, eventually performing a play written by the African children.

In the live arts there has also been a significant development of partnership projects: companies of actors – professional companies, youth theatres and community groups – from different cultures creating collaborative work: re-working the classics (Shakespeare, The Mahabharat), making new plays, staging dramatic events that combine the experiences of different cultures.

All of the above are evidence that 'globalisation' need not be simply about the shifting of commodities, services and the workforce around the world in more cost-efficient ways (cost-efficient, that is, from the standpoint of the multinational corporations). Which is not to say that governments do not have a keen interest in the aspects of schools twinning projects that are about economic growth and the future balance of payments. But collaborations between cultures do seem to tap into a need to alleviate – and indeed challenge – the worst aspects of a global economy that is still based upon an unfair distribution of wealth and an aggressively competitive national and individual identity.

PRACTICAL ASPECTS OF A TWINNING PROJECT

The work in this book is another example of how creative interaction between different cultural groups can operate. The process offered here takes such activity to another level – the creation of new work that develops from a collaborative process between groups of young artists from different cultures or communities. Embedded at the very heart of this process is the challenge that such collaborative intercultural work presents to the non-plastic brain – those evolved structures that seek to control and manipulate the environment, and that tend to put up barriers between 'us' and 'the other'.

The scope and scale of your own project will be unique to your own context. You will find ways to adapt the work in the book to your own purposes. But there are some guiding principles that apply to all projects, and so it may be useful at this point to look at some of the practical aspects of setting up, steering and managing such a project. They are given here as general guidance, that you will adjust according to the nature of your project.

The agenda of the project

Whatever the nature, context and scope of your project, the practicalities should be rooted in the agendas that are at the heart of the book:

• You are seeking a *partnership of differences*. Whether your project is local, regional, national or international, its value is rooted in placing two diverse groups in a creative dialogue with each other. The differences may be ones of ethnicity, culture, language, community, gender, sexuality or class. It is through this diversity that you will discover the unique creative nature of your project. I have already referred to a project I was involved with that twinned an inner-city, mixed-race school with an all-white rural school. The creative dialogue that developed – and the work that was produced – could only have come from this partnership of difference. There will be challenges. Local or regional 'rivalries' may assert themselves to begin with. Inter-ethnic or class differences may be apparent. A lesbian and gay youth group will present their own challenges to a group that does not define itself as such (and vice versa). But these challenges are the 'grit that produces the pearl': the creation of fresh, new work that flows from the dialogue of diversity.

- The project should be *youth led* to the greatest degree possible. This is not to say that the young artists involved should not be in collaboration with older colleagues (mentors, guides, youth workers or teachers). But the aim of the project goes far beyond simply 'putting on a show'. It is about the development of the *whole person*, and the decision-making process should be in the hands of the young participants as fully as your context allows. This presents a challenge to older collaborators who are working in formal educational structures (or indeed to those of us who are older professional theatre-makers who might feel we 'know all the answers'). But the sense of 'full ownership' of the project by the participants should be as total as can be achieved in the context you are working in.

The scale of the project

Although many of the practical activities in the book are drawn from a large-scale project (*Contacting the World*) they can be applied and adapted to many contexts. With all of these, the core agendas of the project, as mentioned above, should be the guiding principle. The notes below include brief comments on the nature of some projects.

- *Local projects*. The twinning of groups of young people from a particular town or area. These may take place within or alongside formal educational or arts structures, or in a less formal context. They all have their value. Even within a very specific local area, different youth cultures exist, with very little experience of each other. The 'school up the road' may be as alien as another country. In the UK at the moment there is some public concern about 'youth gang culture'. This is often based upon rivalries (often violent in their nature) between groups of young people existing in close proximity to each other. A knee-jerk reaction of 'the authorities' is to 'crack down', but there is evidence that other approaches are possible and possibly more useful. The creative energies that go into destructive or antisocial behaviour (and they *are* creative, even if they manifest themselves in negative ways) can be offered other channels to express themselves.
- *National and inter-regional projects*. The twinning of groups of young people from different regions – within a nation or between adjacent geographical regions. Within the UK, different regional histories, dialects and loyalties

can be as foreign as the other side of the world. Creative projects have not 'dissolved' the differences, but have paved the way for discovering common ground. In the Israel–Palestine region there have been projects that have linked groups of young people from both sides of the divide in creative collaboration.

- *International projects.* The twinning of groups of young people from different cultures around the world. The 'received' and 'perceived' notions of 'other places' can be a starting point for a true discovery. One young British Asian woman involved in a twinning with a company in South Asia said, 'What was weird was, they knew far more about *us* than we knew about *them*. By learning about *them* I learned more about *myself*'.
- *Projects that mix age-ranges.* An older group of young artists working with a younger age-range has its own challenges, but a mutual learning process can result that can be unique. The perceived – and possibly real – inequalities of life-experience may give rise to assumptions, but these are mediated and made complex by differences in culture. Perhaps one of the more challenging types of twinning, this can raise the question of 'Who teaches and who is taught?'.
- *Inter-language projects.* Projects where there is no shared language, or where the groups elect to work in their first language.
- *Short-term or long-term projects.* An exchange of several weeks or a couple of months can – if set up and managed skilfully – achieve as much as a longer-term project. It is important not to see a short project as 'lesser' than a longer one.
- *Multi-twinned projects.* The *Contacting the World* international project twins twelve groups (six pairs of twins), all engaged in the same process, over a nine-month period. Such a project demands greater organisation – and possibly resources – but such a model could also be applied locally, regionally or nationally.
- *'Agenda-based' projects.* Projects that are linked to, or framed by, a particular major event or enterprise – local, national or international. The first *Contacting the World* in 2002 was launched as part of Cultureshock, the north-west UK cultural programme for the XVII Commonwealth Games in Manchester. Six UK youth companies were twinned with six youth companies from the Commonwealth. In 2004 the second *Contacting the World* was produced in partnership with the British Council as part of its Connecting Futures initiative. The particular focus was on forging links with Muslim cultures and communities. Other framing agendas may be more local, such as an initiative to address youth gang culture; or 'topic-based', such as addressing global warming.

With all of the above, and the last in particular, any 'framing agenda' for the project should not override or constrain the ethos of the youth-led nature of the work.

Practical approaches and guidance on the above can be found in Chapter 10.

Finding your twin

The scope and scale of your project will suggest 'where to look and what to look for'. This may happen in a number of ways. The following comments and thoughts may be useful.

- *Who do you know?* Imagine that you and your group have decided that a twinning project is just the sort of thing you'd like to undertake. It might be that you decide it will be a local project, or one with a wider scope – national or international. Whatever it is, it will be something that you have the time, resources and enthusiasm for. Somewhere 'out there' will be the twin you are seeking. To locate them might at first seem a daunting task, but bear in mind that it *might not be as hard as it seems*. Why not start from what, or who, you know? What connections might you have with another school, youth group or arts organisation in your area? If you are in India and want to twin with a group in the UK (or vice versa), does anyone in the group have a link with a school, a community or an arts project in that country? Does anyone have a relative or a friend who might have suggestions? This can apply to both the small-scale and large-scale project. With the first *Contacting the World* project (twelve international groups), the small team of people simply began with lists of everyone (groups and individuals) they had worked with, had contact with or were friends with.
- *Widening the search*. Have you heard or read in the newspaper about a school, a community project or a youth arts project that captures your imagination? Use the Internet to broaden the detective work (the British Council educational twinning projects, for example). Ask the advice of companies or groups that have been involved in other twinning projects (the list of previous *Contacting the World* groups at the end of this book, for example). Find theatre companies that have international connections (the Royal Court in London, for example). Track down officers in local arts-funding bodies who might give a lead.
- *Remember 'the partnership of difference'*. You are not looking for 'like'. It may seem safer to look for a twin whose profile you identify with (a seeming 'suitability'), but that will defeat the object of the exercise. The creative work will be very much based upon 'negotiation between different worlds', so don't be afraid to embrace that difference.
- *Avoid ticking boxes*. Don't go for 'difference' simply because it seems the politically correct tactic, or because you calculate that it will appeal to funding bodies. It is crucial that your particular twinning derives from a genuine enthusiasm.
- *Enthusiasm is all*. You are indeed looking for a twin group that is different from your own – in terms of culture, ethnicity, class, age, experience etc. But beyond all of this, there must be an enthusiasm for the project. As one young artist from a previous *Contacting the World* project said:

Yes, it is important that we are meeting people with different experiences of the world ... and yes, it is important that we're breaking the mould in who can or cannot make art. But unless there is a genuine passion for the work, then it just becomes an exercise in doing the politically correct thing.

• *Random twinning.* This is only appropriate to certain types of project – possibly larger, multi-group ones, but perhaps others. It is one way to avoid totally the temptation to engineer the partnership into some form of safe 'suitability' ('like' as opposed to 'unlike'). With *Contacting the World*, for example, there is no attempt to twin 'like with like' – it is more a question of putting all the groups into a pot and seeing which pairs come out together. This can be a high-risk strategy and (as some of the comments later in the book will point out) can produce both wonderful opportunities and particular difficulties. The 'leap of faith' that is required with any twinning – however sound it might feel – is immense, and the 'significance of the random' makes the leap even higher. But even when (in my experience) the difficulties of a project have been enhanced by such a method, so have the opportunities.

• *This is not an 'adopting process'.* Without in any way discounting the value of educationally based twinning projects (a school in the UK seeking one in Africa, say), there can be something of a flavour of 'adopting' a 'less advantaged' twin, with all the 'do-good' connotations that has. The process encouraged by this book challenges such a tendency entirely – in that it is about the *equal partnership of difference*. The young people involved in the work are all *artists and theatre-makers*. Although there are different levels of experience, aptitude and ability among artists, there is also an equality of spirit that exists beyond the differences of material or educational circumstance. The rural, low-technology group of young artists in India operates on exactly the same plane of creativity as the technologically sophisticated, urban group in the UK.

Negotiating and managing the process

Once you have located a group to twin with, you will need to establish a method of working that is fair to both sides. By 'fair', I mean a method that takes into account the differences that might exist between the groups – differences of experience, language, technological resources etc. A confident and experienced group might 'buy into' the process faster than a group that is new to such work, and the danger here might be that they may wish to move ahead at a faster rate. A group that is used to working without technological resources may not be able – or wish – to respond to their twin in a rapid 'quick fire' manner. There may be issues of 'diary dates' to take into account – holiday periods, periods of religious observance etc. that impact on the different working patterns of the groups. One group may simply 'get stuck' at any point, or feel they have lost their way.

Some of the following advice, comments and observations will be of use in your setting up of the process.

- *A taster activity.* You have located a potential group to twin with. There is a mutual enthusiasm for embarking on a creative journey together. Before fully entering into this 'marriage', you might wish to have a brief 'engagement', to see if this partnership really could be the one that is best for both parties. Take one of the activities from Chapter 2 and see how it works. Think of it as a 'taster' activity – one that will let you know if the mutual enthusiasm for the project that exists between the two groups is borne out in practice. If it is not, nothing has been lost, and you'll have done something new – there will have been no 'failure'. If it is . . . you have started!

- *A schedule.* Establish a definite schedule for the project that takes into account the diary commitments of the two groups. Holiday periods or periods of religious observance or festival may differ. In the UK, the December holiday period, taking in Christmas and the New Year, can extend to two weeks, during which all activities grind to a halt. The periods of Eid or Ramadan may mean that some groups – or members of those groups – are not available for work on the project. Some groups work on a formal schedule of meetings (once a week, say); others in a more irregular and less formal way. All of these things should be taken into account.

- *The impartial guide.* With your group, you will have agreed on a schedule. You will also be negotiating on a course of activities throughout the pro-cess. These will develop as you go along – the first activities will suggest which ones are the most suitable to take up next. The groups should be strongly encouraged to follow through the activities as agreed, so that the exchange of creative work has an equal balance. With the *Contacting the World* project, a 'third party' exists in the equation. An 'artist facili-tator' has a constant and impartial eye on the process, ensuring that the exchange is happening at a rate, and in a manner, that preserves the equality of input and outcome. This person is neutral and non-directorial in terms of the outcomes of the work. Such an 'impartial guide', in the form of a person, may not be possible for some projects, but all the same it is important for the groups to have some equivalent – which is a key function of this book. Use it always to refer back to *what has been agreed upon.* And when – as I hope you will – you diverge from the work in the book as you go along, always *agree on the nature of the divergence.*

- *A contract.* This sounds a little strict, but it can be useful for the groups to commit to the project in a formal wording. Indeed, the negotiating of that formal commitment can be seen as part of the youth-led process: an agree-ment that is not imposed, but that the participants have devised together.

- *Managerial infrastructure.* We live in a rather 'over-managed' world (there seem, these days, to be more arts-officers than artists, more managers in the worlds of the health and education services than teachers or nurses). Any twinning project will need 'managing', of course, but even the most ambitious and large-scale ones can do without cumbersome management infrastructures. Indeed, the smaller the better – as the experience of *Contacting the World* has borne out. As Julia Turpin (Project Director) says, '*Contacting the World* was a big, global project, but we didn't need an over-staffed office to make it work, just a few of us with energy, passion and purpose'. The guiding principle might be: 'keep it small and keep it in the hands of the artists as far as possible'. Here again, the youth-led focus of the project should be the key: planning, scheduling, budgeting, marketing etc. should involve the participants as far as possible.
- *The pastoral aspect of a process.* Any project will be about far more than just 'putting on a show'. It will be about the development of the whole person. Participants will be bringing into the project their whole lives – past, present and future. So, however the project is managed, try to bear this in mind and include in your practice ways of addressing issues that do not seem to relate immediately to the actual work.

KEY CHALLENGES

I hope that is now clear that what might seem to be possibly uncomfortable or difficult *challenges* for your project are in fact key *opportunities*. Here are some of the things you might like to think about as you proceed through the book and the practical work. I will refer back to them as we progress through the chapters.

- *The predominance of English as an international language.* There is (unfortunately) an assumption made here in the UK that 'everyone speaks English'. There is also, in other cultures, the real or perceived need to learn English. The combination of the two can translate into a twinned project being allowed to lean towards English as the common vocabulary. That can seem the easiest route. But those of us who have English as our first language, and those who wish to learn English as a second language, need to think about the implications of that for our projects. A diversity of languages (like species of plants or animals) is disappearing from our planet at an alarming rate, and as artists (who should value diversity of expression) we should be seeking ways to combat that. So a first big question for any cross-cultural project must be, 'How do we create this work together without it being another step towards the predominance of English as *the* accepted channel for the expression of ideas through words?' As I write here – in English – I'm aware that, in hoping this book may be of use to groups who do not have English as a first language, it's a good example of the very thing I'm wanting us to avoid. Given that contradiction, I hope that I can express my thoughts – in English – as clearly and precisely as possible, in a manner that does not *assume* you know what I'm thinking and that you can translate into your own languages (my challenge and my opportunity).

- *The challenge of translation.* If we do take on board the use of multiple languages in our projects, then we are going to have to deal with translation. And 'translation' is not just the technical substitution of one word or phrase from one language into another. Words are loaded things – symbols for deep cultural meanings and assumptions. In my own culture, the words 'black' and 'white' carry huge historical baggage with them. 'Black' is placed in very negative terms ('black as sin', 'black as the devil', 'a black mood' etc.). 'White' is related to positive images (brides wear white as a sign of purity, soap powder turns your white washing out 'pure white', great innocence is seen as 'whiter than white' etc.). In other cultures, the words 'white' and 'black' can have entirely different signific -cation – 'white as the colour of death', for example, and 'black' as a symbol of pride.

- *The opportunities of translation (1).* So the opportunity of the challenge here might be to find a good translator at the start of the project. And that may not be as difficult as it seems. Is there someone you know – a member of the group, a friend, a relative, someone in the community – who is familiar with the language of your twin group? Here is an ideal opportunity to draw in other people to the project – you may not be looking for 'the professional translator', but for someone who might have a sense of the *colloquial* and the *daily* of the new language you are dealing with. The use of live film as a means of communication between the groups can be invaluable, too. As one participant in a multilanguage twin-ning project said, 'To actually see and hear the other group speaking really helped – how the tone of voice and the physical gesture made real sense of what they meant, much more than just the written dialogue on the page'.

- *The opportunities of translation (2).* In the exchange process you will need to find ways of engaging with a twin group that does not share your first language. You may learn some of their language, and even incor -porate that into your final performance. But in terms of your final performance – whatever language or languages you use – there is one, great, liberating opportunity you might consider: *you may not need the words you use to be translated.* Until now, I have referred to 'translation' as a verbal exercise, but we are dealing with *live theatre*, which of all the art forms incorporates all the others. Gesture, tone, movement and dance, pictorial, musical, spatial, architectural as well as the verbal all have equal place in the ritual of theatre. The 'meaning' of a piece of theatre can lie in all or any of these, but we should not assume that the verbal is necessarily predominant. Some theatres (often opera) have adopted the strategy of 'surtitles' on an electronic screen to translate for the audience the words that are being spoken, and 'audio-description' has been developed to aid audience members who are sight-impaired. Both of these (certainly the latter) have their uses in conveying aspects of a performance to audience members. But in terms of the language you are using, should you elect to work in one that is unfamiliar to your audience, do not be afraid to do so. A group from Syria, performing at one of the *Contacting the World* festivals in the UK, used their own language throughout, and, far from that being a problem for the audience, it was entirely appropriate. The 'meaning' of the play was conveyed through the combination of mood, atmosphere, stage picture, lighting, tone and gesture. There was absolutely no need to 'translate' the specifics of the dialogue.

- *Perceived and actual cultural inequalities.* I have already mentioned that we should avoid the rather patronizing 'adopting' attitude to twinning – a sort of 'doing good' to folk we think of as less fortunate than ourselves. The school in Africa may not have access to the benefits of technology. The rural community group in the north of England may not be 'culturally sophisticated'. A younger-age twin partner group may be perceived as 'having less to say'. But if the heart of the project is truly 'the twinning of difference' – of experience, history, thought and imagination – then we are on a level playing field, starting from the view that 'we are all artists'.

- *Negotiating difference.* Following on from the above, we must find ways of negotiating with sensitivity and bravery such issues as different faiths and world-views. We may be working with a culture that has attitudes towards certain things that we do not share – the place and position of women in society, the response to different sexual orientations, the role of the male in society, the place of religion in the culture, for examples. We may discover things about our twin that puzzle, perplex, confuse or even shock us. But here again is the great opportunity to re-assess our own views of the world in the light of other ways of thinking about it. This does not mean that we cannot challenge views that we do not share. Such challenges, in a creative context, can enrich the process. Nor should we be over-sensitive about how our twin may receive our own views and feelings – as John McGrath says, 'Never decide what other people's sensitivities are going to be, don't place your assumptions as to *what you think may offend* onto your twin'. However, as you proceed, you will discover – often in small but significant ways – things about your twin group and its culture that should be taken on board. I am reminded of an exhibition that a group in the UK was preparing, composed of filmed images of its twin group, to be projected on the walls and floor of their space. Someone pointed out that some of the images were of a religious nature, and that to project them onto the floor would be seen as hugely disrespectful – 'You'll be treading on their culture'.

- *The decolonisation of power relationships.* All of the above relates to this – the historical assumptions we carry with us regarding our relative cultural positions in the world. Here in the UK there is still the tendency to 'carry the Empire around in our heads' and an innate sense of superiority. On the other side, from the previously colonised cultures, there remain the remnants of subservience to (and possible hostility towards) the 'mother country'. Both less so these days, one hopes. So 'decolonisation' is not an issue or a problem just for the previous western empires. And here again – in a creative enterprise – the opportunity is opened up for artists to look at our shared responsibility to address and change the attitudes, practices and symbols that still uphold the 'colonial frame of mind'.

AIMS AND ASPIRATIONS

Depending on the scope and scale of your project, you will devise your list of aims for a twinning project – and the voices and thoughts of the young people and young artists will be central to what you come up with. Below are examples of aims and aspirations as expressed by two different projects.

The Salzburg global seminar

At a recent seminar in Salzburg, the Youth and Education Group included the following in its aspirations for the development of creative work between young people and young artists:

- to establish learning environments where compassion, respect, equity, justice and a global understanding are fostered;
- to allow young people to use the arts to think globally, and to understand the issues of others as relevant to themselves, beyond borders of nationality and identity;
- to see young people as artists of today, not tomorrow, who are legitimate participants in culture;
- to encourage group process – everyone is a teacher.

Contacting the World

The aims for the twinning project are:

- to create mutual understanding and respect between young people from different backgrounds;
- to produce and experience new performance work that reflects cultural and creative diversity;
- to exchange and develop new performance skills, contributing to and enhancing participants' understanding of different practice;

- to integrate an innovative and creative use of new technologies into the theatre-making process;
- to create a sustainable network of young theatre-makers;
- to increase awareness of the range and quality of work being made by young people;
- to provide creative opportunities for the personal development of participants;
- to provide an international platform and profile for theatre made by young people around the world.

The book will now proceed with its creative work. I hope that some of the things in this chapter will have given you some food for thought, as well as some practical advice. If anything in it has seemed not appropriate to your project, or a little daunting, then ignore it for the moment. Come back to the chapter if and when you need to. The main thing now is to embark on a creative journey that is stimulating, nourishing, challenging and *fun*.

A colleague of mine once said, 'The greatest thing about the work – and how we learn and develop best – is when there is laughter in the room'. Bring laughter into your room.

COMMENT

It is best if the two groups are very different – so when you *do* find common ground it really *is* common ground.

(Company member, Contact, UK)

. . . it was the story of two communities with a combined history – the Kasmiri muslim and the Kashmiri pandit. Centuries of living together, of combined landscapes and mindscapes, are interwoven with feelings of hatred, of suffering at each other's hands. It is the story of Neeraj Guatam, a fourteen year old boy from Jammu. He said: 'I had come here full of apprehension, prejudices created by my parents in Jammu. Hatred was just below the surface. But what we got was inqualified love, best expressed in the song we sang together at the end of the performance.

'"Iss desh ko Hindi na musalman chahiye
Agar chahiye to ek achha insaan chahiye."'

(The Pandies, India)

2   A creative dialogue

This chapter will give a range of creative activities that introduce the twinned groups to each other. In choosing which ones to use for your project, bear the following in mind:

- *Select your activities.* It is not necessary to use all the activities: choose the ones that are most suitable to the scope and nature of your project. The first contact between the groups should be engaging and fun, encouraging curiosity and a sense of anticipation for the journey that is ahead. It is most important not to 'overload' each other with work, to the point where it becomes a tedious 'task'.
- *Negotiate with your twin.* Negotiate with your twin as to which activities both groups will use. It is important, in terms of follow-up work, that each group uses the same activities.

    Agree on deadline dates with your twin for the delivery of the results of the work: it is always helpful if both groups receive the results of their twin's activities at the same time.
- As a guide, you might consider two activities: any one from Activities 1–5, plus Activity 7 (recommended as an essential activity for all projects).
- It might be that you wish the 'introductory period' of the process to take place over more than one exchange of activities, in which case you will be able to engage with more of the activities in this chapter.
- Regarding Activity 6, this is slightly more 'cerebral' than the others. It has been used in previous twinning projects as an introductory activity, but might best be used – if appropriate – as a follow-up to the initial activities.
- *Reassure* the group that, in engaging with these activities, no-one should feel the need to 'self-censor'. The object of all the activities is to attempt to be as open as possible, even if that means revealing things that do not show us in a 'best light'. This will become increasingly important as the collaboration between the groups develops: plays are about asking

difficult questions – about ourselves and our world – and the process of making them should not be inhibited by us being 'politically correct'. Before any of the exchange activities take place, it would be useful for the group to have a discussion about this – in a manner that is appropriate to the nature and age make-up of the group.

The function of the activities in this chapter is to:

- provide a clear and imaginative framework for an introductory dialogue;
- encourage all individual voices within each group to participate in the activity;
- enable each group to learn something new about itself as well as share some things with its twin;
- begin to give an 'essence' of the different cultures, histories, countries, regions or localities of the groups.

The activities will encourage participants to ask themselves the following questions:

- How do I express myself – my thoughts, concerns and experiences; my hopes, fears and dreams – to someone I have never met?
- How do I begin to engage with the lives and experiences of people who are strangers to me?
- How do we represent our culture, society and history in a manner that is not 'text book' type information?

The work in this chapter will therefore enable and equip the participants to enter into a creative dialogue that goes beyond the purely 'informational' and is of the heart and the spirit as well as the intellect. By encouraging the participants to reflect as well as to 'do', the work will create a basis for a collaboration that is grounded in empathy and curiosity.

All the work in this chapter will begin to provide material for creative development in the next stages of the project. The cross-reference to activities in following chapters will show the reader how this initial exchange of material is a vital component in building the plays that will eventually take shape.

Activity 1 Postcards

You are going to send your twin group a series of postcards that give an 'essence' of who you are as a group.

Part one – sending your cards

1   Obtain a set of blank postcards. You are going to use these to introduce yourselves to your twin group.

2 Think about the question 'Who are we?' – as a group and as individuals in a group. Ask yourselves the following and make lists. Make sure that everyone in the group has contributed to the lists.

- What are the words or phrases that best describe us? (See Example 1.1.)
- What are the images – line drawings, colours etc – that best represent us? (See Example 1.2.)
- What are the most important things we would like the world to know about us?

3 Keep the lists you have made for future reference.

4 Once you have full lists, find satisfying ways of putting the results on to one side of the postcards. Bear in mind the following:

- The words and phrases are not meant to sum up everything about you: think of them as 'snapshots'.
- Do not worry if the results – particularly the images (see examples below) – seem obscure or do not 'explain' themselves.
- Decide how many postcards you want to use and how they will be used.
- You might have one postcard each for every member of the group, or work in small teams with a postcard for each team.
- You might use some postcards for colours or images only, others for words and phrases etc., or combine them.

5 Address the postcards to your twin group and send them.

Part two – receiving their cards

1 Receive the postcards your twin has sent you.

2 Compare the postcards your twin has sent you with the original lists you made:

- Are there any striking similarities of thought, imagery etc.?
- Are there any exceptional differences?
- What would you like to know more about?

Example 1.1 Words and phrases

Here are a few examples from different groups around the world who have engaged in this activity. Note how they all give vivid 'snapshots' of who they are:

- 'We are different people with different ideas, coming together for the common purpose of sharing art.'
- 'We are educating and shaping the world.'

- 'We are many and varied in our make-ups.'
- 'We are "international", "individual", "explorers", "communicators", "creative", "passionate", "welcoming".'
- 'We are a new group of young artists who aim to create exciting new work.'
- 'We are prosperous, we are winners, we aim at being prosperous in all ways.'

Example 1.2 Images

Here are a few descriptions of images from around the world that were sent by groups engaging in this activity. Note how they are all quite abstract.

- A person (half woman and half man) with many arms holding different musical instruments.
- A multicoloured zebra with huge eyes wearing a jester's hat, riding on a magic carpet over a bridge.
- A clock-tower/rocket taking off. Diwali lights festooned across the top of it, with two stick people: one boy and one girl, with the word 'Diverscity' (*sic*) making up their stick arms and legs.

Outcome

Rather like the proverbial 'message in a bottle', washed up from a distant shore, the postcards have given a brief insight into the life and experience of each group. They will hopefully have intrigued the recipients and aroused the desire to know more. What they have left out will have been as important as what they included: the function is not to 'explain', rather to arouse curiosity and prompt questions.

Cross-reference

See Activities 13 and 56.

Activity 2 Filling the box

This activity has a similar function to the first one, but has a more 'tactile' quality to it.

Part one – sending your box

1 Obtain a cardboard box (shoebox size, or something similar).
2 You are going to put a number of items (no more than ten) into the box, which will then be sent to your twin.

3 The items will give an impression of the environment you live in ('our world') – be that your community, locality, district, region or country of residence.

4 Each item will have some significance to you as a group: that is, it will 'say' something important about the part of the world you share as a group.

5 The items should 'speak for themselves': that is, they do not have to be accompanied by an explanation.

6 The items should draw upon as many of the five senses as possible: sight, sound, touch, taste, smell. So you might include:

   • printed text, articles and newsprint, leaflets, photos, film etc.;
   • music tapes and CDs, sound recordings etc.;
   • found or made objects etc.;
   • sweets, flavourings, biscuits, etc.;
   • herbs, perfumes etc.

7 Depending on the size of the group, there will be some negotiation necessary to agree on those items that represent most fully the shared world of the group.

8 The *limitations* of the size of the box and the number of items are important. This would suggest that the items should be of a hand-held size.

9 What you are seeking to give your twin is an *essence* of your world, not the whole of it. Do not worry if you have not covered all aspects: 'intrigue' rather than 'explain'.

10 When you have selected your items, post the box to your twin. It would be worth remembering – if you are sending the box overseas – to check any customs restrictions and regulations etc.

11 Keep a record of the items you have included for future reference.

Part two – receiving their box

1 Receive the box your twin has sent you.

2 Compare the items your twin has sent you with the record of the ones you sent your twin:

   • Were there any striking similarities between the items sent and received?
   • What were the greatest differences between the things sent and received?
   • What items prompt curiosity in you – which ones do you have questions about?

Example 2.1

Here are some examples of items included in boxes sent by groups from around the world who have engaged in this activity. Note how they are very specific, but do not necessarily 'spell out' what their particular 'significance' is.

*   A tin container from a bottle of Glenfiddich (Scottish) whisky.
*   Yesterday's local newspaper from a town in the north of England.
*   A sample of rattan leaves, used during rituals to drive away bad spirits.
*   A mixed soundtrack of daily life in South Africa.
*   A photo of a railway information board in England, with all the trains having been cancelled.
*   A photo of a dead seagull, covered in oil.
*   Some chilli powder.
*   Some locally made sweets.
*   A folk tale from South Asia.
*   A bar of scented soap.
*   A seashell.
*   A bank statement.
*   Train tickets.
*   A poster from India of a Bollywood film.
*   A packet of sand.

Example 2.2

An *adaptation* of this activity might be the inclusion of *agreed* items in the box. A twinning project between a school in the UK and one in Brazil agreed that the main items would consist of masks made by the children.

> The most exciting moment was when the parcel from Brazil was unwrapped in the classroom in Hackney. The layers of brown paper were ripped open as though it was everybody's birthday and the masks came tumbling out. They included materials such as tropical leaves and grasses which, combined with the vibrant coloring, gave a real sense of the culture and landscape. The children put the masks on and each were instantly transformed by the power of the mask. Spontaneously, the 50 year old teacher and the 10 year old children began to jiggle, twirl, dance and strut. We all traveled to another place in our bodies and imagination. These masks were used in the final performances.
>
> (Michael Judge, Theatre Centre, UK)

Outcome

You and your twin group have already begun to tell each other stories. Behind every item in the boxes is a complex of history, culture, daily life and experience. The box you have received can be regarded as a 'creative gift', and its contents go beyond a simple 'getting to know you' exercise: they have provided material that will begin to inspire the making of your play. At the moment, many of the items may seem mysterious or perhaps of little significance, but – as we shall see later – they can become a rich source of material for the creative process.

Cross-reference

See Activities 14–15, 53 and 57.

Activity 3 On this day

In this activity you are going to give your twin group an insight into a typical day in the lives of the members of your group.

Part one – your day

1   Agree on a specific day with your twin.

2   On the agreed date, each member of your group will make an individual account of his or her day's activities.

3   The account can be made in any number of ways, in whatever manner or form each person feels comfortable with:

- • a formal written diary;
- • a list of things done or accomplished;
- • a list of usual routines and new challenges;
- • an account of successes or failures;
- • a poem;
- • a 'map' of the day, showing the routes taken and drawings of the major events, changes of direction, obstacles etc.;
- • a sequence of photographs (with or without captions);
- • a recorded documentary – audio or filmic.

4   Send your twin group the final accounts.

5   Retain copies of your own accounts for future reference.

Part two – their day

1   Receive the accounts sent by your twin.

2   Compare the accounts sent by your twin with your own.

- Are there any striking similarities?
- Are there any significant differences?
- Are there any particular daily routines, activities etc. mentioned by your twin group that intrigue, puzzle or alarm you?
- Is there a general pattern of activities that links the individual experiences mentioned by your twin group?
- Is there a general pattern of activities that links the individual experiences of your own group?

Example 3.1

Here are a few examples of how the activity was approached by a range of individuals from different twinning projects:

- A group from London drew maps of their area. As the day progressed they wrote down 'significant things' that had happened to them at points on the map. Some of the events were minor ('I found a coin on the pavement'), some of more serious consequence ('I missed the bus because I had forgotten to get a ticket from the machine') and some quite self-revealing ('I was deliberately rude to the person in the shop').
- A person from Malaysia took a series of photographs of different clocks at different times of the day.
- A person in England turned her 'first person' diary into a 'third person' short story ('She woke up late and never had time for breakfast. Then she rang her best friend and arranged to meet in the local park, but she never made it because . . .').
- A group in India drew portraits of everyone they had met that day.

Outcome

You will now have begun to form a picture of your twin, not just as a group, with its own identity and a world it inhabits, but as a collection of distinct individuals. This will be important to remember as you continue with the collaboration – each group may have its own identity, but within it are uniquely individual voices.

Cross-reference

See Activity 16.

Activity 4 Food for thought

Food – and the customs, activities, rituals, preparation and consumption of it – is something that we all share (in our different societies). In this activity you are going to use this universal topic to learn more about your twin – and yourselves.

Part one – your thoughts

1   Agree on a mutually convenient week with your twin.

2   During the week, each member of your group will write an account of some of their activities related to eating, meals, food etc. These accounts may include some or all of the following:

- types of food eaten;
- when, where and with who were meals taken?
- the etiquette of eating;
- favourite foods and dishes;
- fast food or home cooked food?
- if cooked food, who did the cooking?
- recipes;
- meals for special occasions, events, rituals, festivals etc.;
- fasting, special diets, 'forbidden foods';
- regional and cultural specialities;
- global and local foods;
- the cost of food;
- where and how was the food you ate produced?

3   Retain your lists for future reference.

4   Send your twin the results.

Part two – their thoughts

1   Receive the accounts written by your twin group.

2   Compare your lists with those of your twins:

- Are there significant differences?
- Are there similarities?
- Are there items of food that are unfamiliar to you?
- Are there events and festivals including eating and meals that are new to you?

Example 4.1

Here are a few examples of some of the different responses to 'food thoughts' included in accounts from around the world:

- a description of a South African 'brie' (barbecue) party;
- a description of a children's birthday party at a McDonald's restaurant;
- a recipe for traditional Lancashire hotpot (stew);

- a full account of a week's worth of till receipts from a supermarket;
- a quotation from a Victorian 'good table-manners' instruction book;
- the 'air-miles' journeys of various items of food that were eaten during the week;
- a recipe for the best way to cook rice;
- an account of how a period of religious fasting works;
- instructions on how to grow herbs and what their uses are;
- a day-to-day record of school meals;
- a list of items of 'fast food' eaten 'on the hoof' (walking down the street);
- a description of a traditional South Asian vegetarian meal.

Outcome

You will now have a picture of a 'week in the life' of the people you are twinned with, from a very specific angle. You may have learned of types of food, customs and rituals that are new to you. All this can provide rich source-material for incorporation into your own creative work.

Cross-reference

See Activity 17.

Activity 5 Completing the phrase

This activity will enable the individuals in the groups to reveal something of their 'inner lives'. In the process of making new theatre together, the ability – based on mutual respect and trust – to place 'the personal' at the heart of the work is essential.

Part one – your phrases

1   Working individually, each member of the group completes the following phrases:

- 'I love . . .'
- 'I wish . . .'
- 'I don't understand. . .'

2   Place the results of everyone's work in three lists, under the three headings.

3   Retain a copy of your own lists for future reference.

4   Send the list of results to your twin group.

Part two – their phrases

1   Receive the list sent by your twin group.

   • Are there any similarities between your lists and those of your twin?
   • Are there differences?
   • Which phrases are about very *personal* things; which are about *wider* issues?

2   Make one long list of all the results – yours and your twin's.

Example 5.1

Here are some examples of completed phrases from different groups from around the world who have undertaken this activity:

1   *'I love . . .'*

   • I love all my ex-girlfriends.
   • I love politics.
   • I love the knowledge.
   • I love the winter.
   • I love Manchester United football club.
   • I love all who can be loved.
   • I love making random sentences.
   • I love my soul and myself.

2   *'I wish . . .'*

   • I wish it were the school holidays.
   • I wish my grandmother was still alive.
   • I wish it would rain.
   • I wish I could see into the future.
   • I wish I had a pet dog.
   • I wish there was no war.
   • I wish my tooth did not ache.
   • I wish the world would grow up.
   • I wish to do acting till my death.
   • I wish I didn't have such strong opinions about everything.

3   *'I don't understand . . .'*

   • I don't understand electronics.
   • I don't understand the severe security in front of the American Embassy.
   • I don't understand narrow-minded people.
   • I don't understand why I'm not a superstar in Hollywood.
   • I don't understand the point of this exercise.
   • I don't understand maps.

- • I don't understand myself.
- • I don't understand society and their morals and ways.
- • I don't understand ladies.

Outcome

You will now have some insight into the great variety of thought and feeling that exists within the twinned groups. There will have been significant similarities (who supports the same football teams?), some personal insights (teeth that ache, missed grandmothers) and some challenging opinions (why does the world need to grow up?).

One of the 'I wish' responses gives us an excellent example of one aspect of the process that will come up later in the book: the 'unexpected'. That is, something that sparks off a completely new activity – one that you have not come across in the book, but that inspires you to develop the thought. The phrase is '*I wish it would rain*'. Here is a great opportunity to create an exchange around the responses to *the weather* in different cultures. For instance, people in parts of Bangladesh or Mexico recently (and even parts of the UK in the summer of 2007) were certainly not wishing it would rain – flooding has ruined lives, communities and crops. In other parts of the world, where drought is frequent, the wish for rain will be very strong indeed. In this one simple phrase, opportunities for a whole range of work are suggested: stories where 'the weather' is a central 'character' in the narrative.

So a major learning outcome for all groups here is: be on the lookout for the unexpected or accidental clues in the work for creating your own activities.

Cross-reference

For further use of this activity, see Activity 18.

Activity 6 Questions

As mentioned at the beginning of this chapter, this activity – depending on the nature of the collaboration and the groups involved – might not have its best place in the very initial introductory work. If that is the case, it could be used as a secondary 'follow-up' introductory activity.

In the examples for Activity 5, one completed phrase was 'I wish I didn't have such strong opinions about everything'. Aside from this being a rather brave and self-examining statement, it gives us a door into an important aspect of making a piece of theatre – particularly one that is being created collaboratively. 'Opinion' in itself is not a bad thing – strongly held ideas and beliefs that can be strongly defended and equally strongly argued against are a necessary part of our development as individuals and groups. However, when we come to certain activities – such as making plays – we need to find ways of stepping outside forms of 'opinion' that might seem over-rigid or 'stuck'. Politicians offer their opinions ('such-and-such is the problem') and then give us their solutions ('such-and-such is the answer to the problem'). A play, on the other hand, if it is going to involve and challenge its audience, works in another way entirely – generally by showing us *human behaviour in action* and asking *questions that are hard to answer*. For example, in James Baldwin's play, *Blues for Mister Charlie*, set in the southern states of America, he shows us how people line up on different sides of the racial divide; what he does not do is give us a text-book answer on how to 'cure' racism. He asks difficult questions about how we can behave as human beings, but does not provide a solution.

In the collaborative twinning process – the meeting of two groups of people from possibly very different backgrounds and cultures – there may well be strong differences of opinion, belief and tradition in evidence. As mentioned earlier in this chapter, it will be important not to side-step these or 'brush them under the carpet': we are not in the business of being 'politically correct' or 'being polite to each other'. That is not to say, of course, that we are seeking unhelpful or uncreative confrontations – far from it – but we are encouraging each other to be as open and as honest as possible.

Therefore, it may be useful – at an early stage in the collaboration – to encourage the development of a good 'questioning' habit: that is, questions that possibly challenge our notions of self, identity and belief; questions that do not have a simple answer, but that provoke us – and our audiences – to consider, through the dramas we are making, the world we share.

1   Each group will prepare lists of questions. Ideally, they should be 'open questions' – that is, questions that are not just seeking a point of technical information ('How many people live in Bangladesh?' or 'Do you live in a house or a flat?').

2   The questions can be in a range of categories:
    • questions about myself;
    • questions about my society;
    • questions about the world.

3   When framing the questions, it is important not to be thinking about what the 'answers' might be: just ask the questions.

4   Initial work on the questions may be done individually. After that, the group can negotiate on perhaps *three questions* from *each category* to send to their twin.

5   Each group will then have eighteen questions: nine of their own, nine of their twin's.

Example 6.1

1 *Questions about myself*:
   - Why do I always have such strong opinions about everything?
   - What do I really believe?
   - What is the best advice I could give to someone who is unhappy?

2 *Questions about my society*:
   - What is the secret of a happy land?
   - How could everyone be equal?
   - Why is there injustice?

3 *Questions about the world*:
   - Where is the world going?
   - Can animals have rights?
   - What would God have to say about the world today?

Outcome

Each group will now have similar lists of 'big questions'. They address personal concerns, concerns about the immediate world of the participants, concerns about the wider world. In contrast to some of the very specific things that have been shared in the other activities (images, items, objects, thoughts etc.), the lists will give a sense that the groups now share a range of questions that go beyond the details of everyday life; big, universal questions that might begin to inform the plays that are being made.

Cross-reference

See Activities 19, 37–38, and 53.

COLLABORATIVE ACTIVITIES

At the heart of the twinning process is the philosophy of collaborative activity: between the members of the groups involved, and between the groups. This aspect of the work will be developed throughout all the chapters, but it is worth noting that it is most useful at the very outset of a project – to engage the group with the notion of 'collaboration'.

Activity 7 A non-theatre collaboration

Each group is to engage in an activity that is not specifically about 'making theatre', but that requires the group to work together on something that is enjoyable, useful and engaging and which – most importantly – involves all members of the group in the sharing of the task. This might seem an obvious point to make, but it is worth remembering that many young people are developing themselves in a world that often places stress on 'individual achievement' as opposed to 'group endeavour'. It can often be very confusing to step out of the world of 'individual success–failure' (tests, exams, job interviews etc.) into that of making theatre, which – even in its most traditional form – is essentially a collaborative activity. So, if we are working with a group over a period of time, there can be great benefits to be had from developing the 'collaborative habit'.

The nature of the group and the scope of the project will determine what type of activity or activities are most appropriate or possible. A school-based group, for example, might devise a team-based enterprise to spend a day 'making the school a better place to be in'. One project decided to arrange a visit to a rest home for the elderly and engage in a range of 'shared stories' activities.

1   Decide with the group what your non-theatre collaboration will be.

2   Make sure that everyone has an equal role in the process.

3   *Exchange* with your twin the result of your activity. Choose the form of 'report back' that feels most useful and engaging.

Example 7.1

A group in New Zealand – twinned with a UK group – decided to combine their opening of the 'filled box' (Activity 2) with this task. This is how they described it in their report-back:

> We got your shoe box today and we opened it in combination with our non- theatre collaborative task. We had a shared meal in a favourite spot . . . we had previously each put a favourite place to meet and a shared meal (like a picnic) into a hat . . . we then picked out one of those and it was Ashley's favourite place . . . at Mission Bay eating fish and chips . . . Mission Bay is about 20 minutes by car from the central city around the waterfront . . . Auckland is surrounded by water . . . we have 2 harbours and Mission Bay is in the Waitemata Harbour . . . it is very beautiful and as we are going into summer it's a very popular place for people to walk, swim, run, eat meals etc . . . you look out at Rangitoto, a beautiful island (one of many in the harbour). We ate our dinner there on picnic blankets . . . before that we opened your box and it was amazing – the first thing we saw was a photo of a boy with 'Liquor she'll love it' and Misi, one of our members, was wearing the exact same shirt . . . same colour and everything . . . we just laughed and laughed . . .
>
> (Massive, New Zealand)

Here are some examples of non-theatre collaborative activities that Fabio Santos and Diane Thornton (Artist Facilitators for *Contacting the World*) engaged in with groups they have worked with. They give an inspirational picture of the range of activities that are possible:

- working with a group of elderly ladies from a community in Brazil to cook Sunday meals for homeless children;
- working with young people to investigate the lives of two culturally, socially and economically distinct families in South Africa living across the road from each other;
- making fancy dress costumes with a group of friends, dressing up and driving in convoy for two hours to visit another friend in hospital; when we arrived we sang a song we had written for him to make him laugh;
- creating a multimedia piece with a team of artists and young students from Palestine, and later screening their film to the students of the same age in Glasgow.

Another example was an activity carried out by Tiyatro 0.2, Istanbul. It was to increase the sales of a stall-holder selling chestnuts. This involved music, interaction with the public and distributing stickers. The sales were increased.

Outcome

Your 'non-theatre' collaborative activity will have helped to create a 'climate' of sharing, team-work, group endeavour and bonding that can only benefit the work of making theatre. Less pressured than 'the rehearsal room', the activity may bring out hidden skills and talents in individuals and encourage the less confident members of the group to be more proactive.

By sharing the results of this activity with your twin group, you will – as we have seen with the example from New Zealand – have given them new insights into who you are and the world you inhabit.

Cross-reference

See Activity 44.

Activity 8 A collaborative theatre activity

Each twin will engage in at least one theatre-making activity that is collaborative in its nature.

Once again, make sure that everyone has an equal role. This does not mean that – in the course of the activity – there are no 'leadership moments'. But it is essential that everyone in the group has the experience of 'taking the lead' at points during the activity.

It may be that your group already has experience of such activities. You might choose a tried-and-trusted favourite activity and adapt it to suit the project, or devise an entirely new one for the project. Whatever choice you make, remember that the project is all about taking new risks, trying new things out and challenging yourselves to 'go further'.

1   Decide what your activity is and carry it through.
2   Record the activity – how it worked in a step-by-step process (see Example 8.1).
3   *Exchange* the results with your twin.

Example 8.1

Here is an example of a collaborative theatre activity that was chosen as a 'favourite' by a group from New Zealand:

> Cat and Mouse. You work in pairs. One person has their eyes covered (the Mouse). The other person is the 'seeing one', and is the 'controller' (the Cat). The 'controller' (or guide) calls out instructions: 'forward . . . stop . . . right . . . stop . . . etc.' Some people in the group use their home language (Maori or Samoan) for their instructions.
>
> After having worked in pairs, form two circles. The outer-circle is made up of the 'controllers' (the Cats). The inner circle is made up of the Mice. Everyone faces into the centre of the circle.
>
> The game is for the Cats to send their Mice into the circle (using their instructions). The Cats follow. The object is for the Cats to catch someone else's Mouse – and avoid their own Mouse being caught.
>
> When a Cat catches a Mouse, the game stops and the Mouse is removed. The game continues until all the Mice are removed.
>
> The game is played again, with Cats and Mice reversing their roles.
>
> (Massive, New Zealand)

Cross-reference

See Activities 43 and 44.

Activity 9 A collaborative day

This activity takes its inspiration from Activity 3 'On this day'. As such, it begins to show us how an activity is not simply a 'stand-alone' task, but can provide a rich source of material for further development and exploration.

Part one – finding the image

1 Look again at the different accounts of the day in Activity 3.

2 Each person in the group chooses one of the accounts – making sure it is not the one that he or she has created.

3 Everyone is going to lead an improvisation.

4 The group stands in a circle. The leader stands outside the circle. He or she takes one short phrase from the day account chosen ('I found a coin on the pavement' for example).

5 The leader speaks the phrase and touches someone (person A) on the shoulder. Person A enters the circle and creates a physical image that represents the phrase. The image can be naturalistic or abstract.

6 The leader repeats the phrase, touching person B on the shoulder. Person B enters the circle and adds to the physical image. This process goes round the circle – persons C, D, E etc. until the whole group has developed a large-scale image.

7 The leader looks at the final image, then moulds the group into a final form. It is important that everyone in the group co-operates with the leader – literally being 'putty in their hands'.

8 The leader takes a photograph of the final image – ideally a Polaroid that can be developed immediately.

9 The group goes back to the circle. The next leader repeats the process with the phrase he or she has chosen.

10 At the end of the process there will be a series of photographs. The leader uses the phrase he or she has chosen to *title the picture*.

Part two – scripting the image

1 Everyone now takes one of the titled pictures – making sure it is not the one they created.

2 Everyone works on their own, with their picture. Guided by the title (the 'major action'), they will produce a short script. There will be a line of dialogue for each person in the picture.

3 The scripts are then handed back to the original leaders of the improvisations.

4 Each leader will then direct the group in a scene. The group stands in a circle again. The leader/director will assign a line of dialogue to each person in the group. The title of the scene is announced, after which the actors can freely improvise the scene – using their one line of dialogue as many times as they like.

5   Having viewed the results of the free improvisation, the leader/director then makes adjustments to the scene, suggesting ways in which it can be developed. They should have a free hand to suggest styles (could the scene be done as a musical, a melodrama or a type of ritual?), who are the lead characters, how it begins and ends etc. It is important that everyone in the group co-operates with the leader/director.

6   This process is repeated with everyone else in the group taking on the role of leader/director.

7   *Exchange* the results of the activity with your twin.

Outcome

•   With both the non-theatre and the theatre-making activities, we have seen how the 'collaborative habit' can be encouraged in the group – among themselves and with non-theatre practitioners.

•   We have seen how every member of the group can have the experience of leadership, and – very importantly – take responsibility for scripting work.

•   The method used in the collaborative day activity could well be applied to the development of other activities – the items in the box in Activity 2 for instance.

Cross-reference

See Activities 43 and 44.

LOOKING FOR INSPIRATION

'Looking', as an inspiration for creating performance, is as important as anything else. We live in an increasingly 'visual' world – TV, film, advertising hoardings, public signs and notices etc – but in the creation of theatre performance it can sometimes be disregarded in favour of 'the word' or 'the idea'.

I was listening to an eye specialist the other day, talking about how – in this 'visual world' – there is a marked increase in the number of eye complaints. He described how the eye muscles needed to be constantly exercised by the activities of (a) 'distant looking' – the horizon – and (b) 'close looking' – immediate detail. Without this interaction, he said, the eye muscles weaken and degenerate. He drew attention to the fact that in our modern world – particularly in crowded, urban environments – there is no horizon: we are generally only looking at the near- or middle-distance. We focus on the people walking towards us, in order not to bump into them. We peer into shop windows or at the tiny images on mobile phones. Buildings cut out any long-distance views. Consequently, our eyesight weakens and degenerates. I thought this was not only an interesting observation from a medical expert on 'how we look' these days, but also a great metaphor concerning a basic human need – to see both the wide horizons and immediate detail of our lives.

So, in our creation of new theatre, we should follow the advice of the medical expert – seek in a metaphorical and a literal way the horizons and the details. The following activities can help us to do that.

Activity 10 Figures in a landscape

It is possible that your twin group will inhabit a different geographical landscape than the one you are familiar with.

One way of starting your project is to use landscape and location as the very first inspiration for your work. That is, to begin with no idea at all as to what story you might develop, but to find your first clues in the physical world around you – by looking.

This is an exercise without words.

1 Work outside. Find a location that is typical or unique to where you live: a field, a park, a beach, a riverbank, a lakeside, a hillside . . . somewhere that has 'a view'.

2 Take account of the time of day, the time of year, what the weather is like.

3 Place some of the members of the group in the landscape. These will be the 'figures in a landscape'. Have them placed separately – single figures in their own space. Don't make any decisions as to why they are there, what they are doing or who they might be.

4 The other members of the group are 'the observers'.

5 Make sure there is a good distance between the 'figures' and the 'observers'.

6 The task of the 'figures' is simply to 'be there'; to interact with the place they are in and allow things to gradually happen; to allow both 'the far' and 'the near' to create impulses of emotion, thought and action.

7 There will eventually be some interactions between the figures, but do not try to push things too hard, don't try to lead the situation or push or anything that is obviously 'dramatic'. Don't worry if nothing seems to be happening. Always keep in mind the landscape you are in – allow it to be a determining feature in what is happening. Think of it as another character – possibly the main one. Allow the natural features of the landscape, the weather and the time of day to be part of the story or stories that evolve.

8   As the situation with the figures evolves, the observers will record it as film or as photographs. 'Instant' photographs or film that can be replayed immediately will be useful.

9   At the end of the process, look at the filmed or photographed results. From the clues given by the 'figures in a landscape', what characters, situations or narratives are suggested?

10 *Exchange* the photographic or filmed results of the activity with your twin. Don't include any of your thoughts about the characters.

11 Receive the results of your twin's experiment. Think about what might be happening, and how the landscape is important to the evolving stories.

12 Try placing yourself in the landscape given to you by your twin.

13 Try an exterior location that is not as open as a landscape – perhaps a little known place, with its own character and history: a disused railway station, an old alleyway, a ruined building.

Cross-reference

See Activities 35 and 54.

Activity 11 Figures in an interior location

As with exterior landscapes, interior locations in your own culture or community may differ from those of your twin – the home, workplace, school etc.

Undertake a similar process to that in Activity 10. In this case, you will be working in a closed environment – but is there still a sense of horizon? What is the view from the windows and how does that affect the outcome of the action? What is the quality of the light coming into the space? If there are no windows and no natural light, what affect does that have on the action?

Outcome

With the landscape and location activities you have:

* enabled your twin group to see more of the world you inhabit;
* shared with your twin ideas about how different landscapes and locations can interact with human behaviour;
* placed yourselves imaginatively within the world of your twin, by suggesting who their characters might be and what they might be doing.

Cross-reference

See Activities 35 and 54.

Plate 1 Workshop, *Contacting the World* 2002.
Photo credit: Matt Squire

Plate 2 Workshop, *Contacting the World* 2006.
Photo credit: John Cooper

Plate 3 Street performance, *Contacting the World* 2006.
Photo credit: Mario Popham

Plate 4 Akshen (Malaysia), *Contacting the World* 2002.
Photo credit: Matt Squire

Plate 5 Performance by Sining Kambayoka Ensemble (The Philippines),
Contacting the World 2006.
Photo credit: John Cooper

Plate 6 Performance by Art of the Street (South Africa), *Contacting the World* 2006.
Photo credit: John Cooper

Plate 7 Kattaikuttu workshop, *Contacting the World* 2002.
Photo credit: Matt Squire

Plate 8 Street Performance, *Contacting the World* 2004.
Photo credit: John Cooper

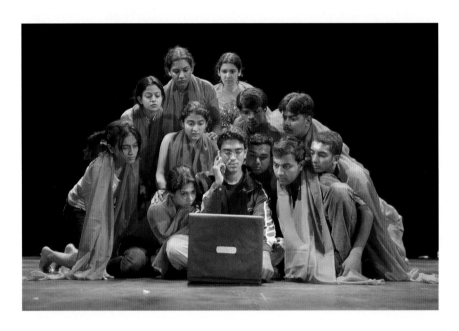

Plate 9 Performance by Project Phakama (India), *Contacting the World* 2006.
Photo credit: John Cooper

Plate 1 Workshop, *Contacting the World* 2002.
Photo credit: Matt Squire

Plate 2 Workshop, *Contacting the World* 2006.
Photo credit: John Cooper

Plate 3 Street performance, *Contacting the World* 2006.
Photo credit: Mario Popham

Plate 4 Akshen (Malaysia), *Contacting the World* 2002.
Photo credit: Matt Squire

Plate 5 Performance by Sining Kambayoka Ensemble (The Philippines),
Contacting the World 2006.
Photo credit: John Cooper

Plate 6 Performance by Art of the Street (South Africa), *Contacting the World*
2006.
Photo credit: John Cooper

Plate 7 Kattaikuttu workshop, *Contacting the World* 2002.
Photo credit: Matt Squire

Plate 8 Street Performance, *Contacting the World* 2004.
Photo credit: John Cooper

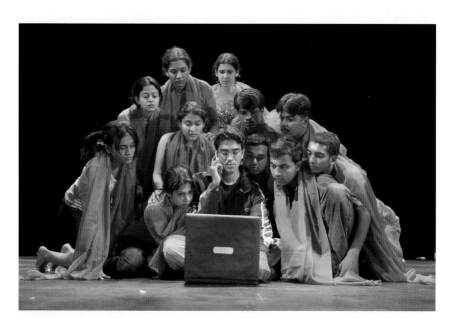

Plate 9 Performance by Project Phakama (India), *Contacting the World* 2006.
Photo credit: John Cooper

PULLING THE THREADS TOGETHER

You will now have entered into a full creative dialogue with your twin. It is worth remembering that everything is going to lead to the creation of a new piece of theatre – one that could only result from the exchange process. What that play will be is not yet clear, but as a final introduction of your group to your twin, you are going to create a 'mini-play' – about five to ten minutes long at most – that draws upon aspects of the shared work so far.

Activity 12 A mini-play

1   Select about twelve things from all the work created so far: key questions, images, characters etc. Remember that this will be a mini-play, so resist the temptation to try to 'get everything in'.

2   Make sure that half the material is from your own work, and half from that offered by your twin (see Example 12.1).

3   Using all the techniques and ways of working that you have explored (and shared) so far, create a short performance that is complete in itself (see Example 12.2).

4   *Exchange* the mini-play with your twin: as a text, as film, as photographs with captions etc.

Example 12.1

Here is a list of things selected at the end of an introductory phase of a project:

- what secret does the moon reveal?
- a burka;
- can we ever really meet each other?
- a group of war-weary soldiers;
- a brick;
- money;
- how do you build?
- why is it broken?
- an old woman sits sleeping on a bench;
- will you sink or will you float?
- a bridge;
- the sound of distant gunfire.

Example 12.2

Here is a summary of how the items from the list were used to inspire a mini performance:

> A woman wearing a burka and carrying a bundle of possessions is crossing a bridge. It is late at night. The middle of the bridge is broken and she cannot get across. On the other side of the bridge is an old woman sleeping on a bench. She is waiting for the woman in the burka. The woman meets a workman who is repairing the bridge. She asks him how long it will be before she can cross it. He holds up a brick, saying that this is the last one and it is not enough to finish the job. She says that she has money enough to pay someone to row her across. He tells her that the waters are too dangerous. A group of soldiers join them. They are in retreat from an invading army. There is the sound of gunfire in the distance. The moon rises. The old woman wakes. She looks towards the bridge. She sees the soldiers and hurries away. The workman hurries home in the opposite direction. One of the soldiers says that the advancing army will be here by midnight. The woman opens her bundle, takes out food and offers it to the soldiers.

Outcome

- By creating a small performance at this stage in the process, you will have experienced how the exchange of creative work can be shaped into a narrative, with characters and a situation.
- By sharing the results of the activity, the twin groups have complete 'mini examples' of how they are developing the skill of adapting the exchanged work.

COMMENT – ASPECTS OF WORK IN THIS CHAPTER

The following comments from previous groups and individuals involved in twinning projects contain some useful critical guidance for any similar project.

No matter how carefully the groups go about communicating with their twin, there will always be times when received material is difficult to work with. If this is seen as an opportunity rather than a problem, then a creative breakthrough can be achieved:

> When we didn't understand our twin, then we danced it out. When we got confused wires, then we moved our bodies and found ways to connect.
>
> (Sining Kambayoka Ensemble, Philippines)

There may be times when the group becomes nervous about a process that – initially – seems not to promise an outcome. The important thing here is to focus on 'the journey' and not attempt to predict the arrival point. 'Keeping open' and trusting the process is key:

> Not knowing what it (our play) was going to be like was half the excitement.
>
> (Colin Simpson, Jackass Youth Theatre, UK)

Although the end result of the process will be plays that have developed through a creative collaboration, it is important to keep in mind the value of the learning that goes on from day one. There will be the time when the demands of putting something together for an audience begin to take precedence, but the 'learning journey' should continue right up to (and indeed after) the moment the performance begins:

> We didn't just work with Art of the Street [South Africa], they brought us into their lives, showed us where and how they live. They educated us, we educated them and we learned together.
>
> (ACT2LDN, UK)

> [T]he project combined well with our company, as it was based in the process of training citizens, not artists. A project like this is essential to promote the interaction between peoples and put a seed of a better future in each participant.
>
> (Victor Porfirio, Novos Novos, Brazil)

Although the twinning project is a creative, as opposed to an academic, venture, there is nothing to be lost from doing some research work into the culture, history, traditions and language of the country or region the group is twinned with:

> The challenge of the collaboration was that the companies should be known better prior to the twinning. We didn't realize that due to language and cultural barriers, our twin company didn't understand what we were writing and they were too polite to say that they didn't understand.
>
> (IFAQ, UK)

'Not knowing' about another culture should not be seen as something to apologise for; but it is important to acknowledge that we may hold stereotypes about it. A key part of the twinning process – the learning that can take place – is to take our limited view of a culture as a given starting point, then see how the journey can deepen and expand our appreciation of the full humanity and creativity of our partners (and indeed ourselves):

[I]t is difficult to think of Rwanda and not of genocide . . . Having recently experienced the death of someone close to me it is impossible for me to contemplate having to cope with acts of genocide . . . The bravery of human beings astounds me . . . I am keen to learn more, but wary of the sensitivities surrounding the topic. I am unsure of how willing people will be to talk about it and their experiences. Maybe they will actively want to? I imagine it is a personal preference, however I would not like to offend or expose difficult emotions . . . it is impossible to know of every taboo and faux pas intwined in the unfamiliar culture. Are there things we take for granted that are not acceptable in Rwanda? I guess my other concern is 'slipping up' in these respects and being unaware. Finding the balance between maintaining respect without appearing to patronize . . .'

(Ruth Cape, Macrobert Youth Theatre, UK)

It was important for us to communicate about New Zealand that we weren't sheep farmers. That we are urban and on the Pacific. Most of all, that it isn't better elsewhere.

(Massive, New Zealand)

When we are working with strangers, linking different cultures, it's very interesting to see how prejudgments come down whilst the process is running forward. In England, I realize youth and children could discover more than violence and football in Brazil. They could discover how happy and controversial Brazilian culture is . . . they could see how the vibrant culture is more than a festival, it could be a movement of resistance and protest as well. Brazilian people, prejudging, think Britain is a very rich country and English people a very 'cold' people. It is surprising to hear, after a project together, how English people are similar to us with their fears and their hopes, and how violent could be relationships in very rich countries as well.

(Joao Andre da Rocha, Nos do Morro, Brazil)

An awareness of your own culture, and the nature of the group you are in, is as important as getting to know and think about the nature and culture of your twin group:

Find as much about your *own* company as possible – that's as important as finding out about your twin. Get to known your *own* group first.

(Company member, Contact, UK)

The choice of activities – and the timing of the exchange – is crucial. Again, the nature of the twins' cultures should be taken fully into account. A group that works mainly with words should not assume that their twin will adapt immediately to that form; a group that meets on a regular basis, working with a twin group that meets on a more occasional basis, might consider a timetable for exchange that allows for that:

> The tasks came too quickly, but we were not in control of when the twin would respond. Also, the tasks were difficult or hard to understand. Some of the tasks were quite writing based and contained conceptual or cognitive ideas. I found that I couldn't respond with the tasks in a physical way. In Africa, it is based on an oral form . . . Black South African Theatre developed against apartheid through non-text based work as a form of protest.
>
> (Art of the Street, South Africa)

Language itself can be a challenge. This book is written in English, which immediately disenfranchises many groups and individuals. If a group whose language is not English, or is part-English, is twinned with an English-speaking group, there will have to be huge creative leaps made, on both sides. Once again, this should be seen as an opportunity rather than a problem:

> Our group has a multi-lingual identity in India and let me assure you that even here at times our audience is not familiar with all the languages used [Hindi, half-Hindi, English, half-English, Punjabi]. The language-challenge [with an India–UK twinning process] bore testimony to the power of theatre to communicate transcending language barriers.
>
> (Pandies, Theatre, India)

> I realized that although I knew what I wanted to say to the twin group, the *way* I was saying it might not be helpful. Don't assume your twin will be familiar with the slang you use. Think about how you are expressing yourself.
>
> (Company member, Contact, UK)

The introductory exchange should set the tone for the project as a whole: discovering what the groups have in common, engaging with cultural differences in a spirit of curiosity, and developing an open critical awareness:

> There are cultural differences, but a lot of the experiences around the world are quite common. There are superficial differences, but the core human experiences we all share. This is not to say that we should state what is right or wrong on stage, but to raise questions that we can all explore as an audience and as performers. Concerning the problem of global intolerance, theatre is important to raise awareness and critical thinking in an audience.
>
> (Companhia Novos Novos, Brazil)

Once an activity has been agreed upon, it is important that both groups follow the same method:

> If you have both agreed to send a set number of objects, then send that number exactly. Adding more stuff because you want to just confuses things. Stick to the rules you've both agreed upon.
>
> (Company member, Contact, UK)

3 Collaborative exchange

In this chapter the creative collaboration between the groups will be broad-ened. Activities – from the previous chapter as well as new ones – will begin to suggest how exchanged material can become the basis for dramatic moments, scenes and dialogues. The guiding principle is that *everything is source material*.

- Activities 13–19 will develop work that was begun in Chapter 2. Material exchanged by the twinned groups in the introductory phase of the project will begin to provide the basis for possible narratives.
- Activities 20–27 will provide new creative-exchange work that also stimu-lates the collaborative 'play-making' process.

Before engaging in the next activities, it might be worth considering some of the following and finding a way of discussing it in a manner that is appropriate to the particular nature and make-up of the group.

This is perhaps *the* crucial stage in the process, where an absolute commitment to, and trust in, the exchanged material are embedded in the work. Collaborative artistic creation does not always come easily – it demands a give and take, a constant negotiation, an ability to listen to the ideas of others and a respect for each other (even when we do not quite agree with or grasp what 'the other' is offering). It is often so much easier to disregard, dis-agree with or belittle what we do not understand. Within a group that we are familiar with – and indeed may have worked with for some time – the individual need to 'be the best' or not to listen to the thoughts of others can interfere with or damage the process. So, when it comes to collaborating with a group of strangers – people we have never met and maybe will not meet face to face for some time – we are posed a double challenge. The 'contact zone' between the groups does not include the 'daily-and-social' interactions we have with our immediate peers and colleagues; nor may it feature the cultural signposts we are used to. The opportunities to disregard, dismiss or disagree with can increase, and so we must work even harder to take what the twin group offers seriously and with respect. This does not mean that we cannot question and challenge, but we can only do this if this is based upon mutual trust and developing empathy.

Key to all of the above is to engage with the creative thoughts and ideas of your twin group as fully and with as much respect as we would wish them to engage with you. The work in this chapter will provide tools for doing so – but there is no chapter in any book that can supply the genuine desire and will to embrace 'the other'; that can only be supplied by the spirit of those engaged in the project.

Activity 13 Dramatic postcards

In Activity 1 the groups exchanged postcards ('Who are we?'). The point was made that the materials sent need not be 'explained' – in fact the ones that are seemingly the most mysterious may be the ones that offer the twin the greatest creative opportunities.

Using some of the material from the postcards, you are going to create something dramatic – an improvisation, an image, a series of images, a dance etc. Think of the material as 'creative clues', not as 'instructions'. The task is to allow the material to inspire you.

1   Look at the postcards your twin group has sent you.

2   Select three specific things from all the material: two phrases and an image, or two images and a phrase for example (see Example 13.1).

3   You can do this as a whole group, or in small teams.

4   Discuss the three things that have been chosen thoroughly. What do they suggest? What might be the best order to place them in? What are the strongest things in the words and the images?

5   Using the three things selected as the focus of your work (the 'spine' or 'theme', if you like), create a dramatic 'moment' that links them together – adding new words and images of your own to flesh out the moment. Use the three things a number of times if that is useful.

6   Do not worry if what you come up with does not seem to make 'sense' – do not be afraid of creating something that is abstract (see Example 13.2).

7   Repeat the process, choosing another three things.

8   Record the work you have created and send it to your twin: as a short script, a filmed piece, a series of photographs with captions etc.

9   Receive the results of the work your twin created from the postcards you sent them.

10 Looking at the ways in which your twin group has used the postcard material you sent them, what new things does that tell you about yourselves? Has your twin seen things in the material that you did not know were there?

Example 13.1

The three selected things from postcards sent by a twin group:

- a phrase: 'We are educating and shaping the world';
- an image: a person (half woman and half man) with many arms holding different musical instruments;
- a phrase: 'We are many and varied in our makeups'.

Example 13.2

The following is an account of a short dramatic piece inspired by the three things. The strong 'clues' in the words and images guiding the piece were 'world', 'shaping', 'educating', 'many' and 'music'.

1   A large inflatable globe of the world is passed around the group. As it passes, the words 'shaping the world' are heard.

2   In the centre of the circle some people are looking at a very large map of the world. There is something underneath the map, moving it and disturbing it, though we do not know yet what it is.

3   Someone stands apart from the group. They have a lump of clay or putty. They pull the lump into different shapes. They are finding the task exhausting. They huff and puff and seem very angry. We hear them saying things such as 'Do as I tell you ... I know what is best for you ... Just listen to me ... I know what is best for you ... etc'.

4   The inflatable globe deflates.

5   The person with the lump of clay has made a perfect ball. They hold it up proudly. They announce to everyone: 'The world must be educated into the shape of perfection'.

6   The large map in the centre of the circle moves in a disturbed way. People around the map start to speak in an overlapping manner – statistics, weather forecasts, environmental disasters, wars etc.

7   There is a loud sound – as of something ripping apart. The large map of the world starts to split. From it emerges many arms, all reaching upwards.

8   Silence.

9   The words 'We are many and various' are heard.

10 The person with the ball of clay says 'There is only one path to perfection'.

11 A figure – both male and female – appears. It has four arms. In each of its hands it holds a different musical instrument.

12 The person with the ball of clay stamps on it.

13   The arms emerging from the large map still reach upwards.

14   People take the musical instruments from the male/female, hold them, as if to start playing.

15   Silence.

16   A short poem is read:

> We are many and varied,
> We have many arms,
> We are shaping the world,
> Many worlds,
> Various worlds.

17   One note of music is heard.

18   The person who has stamped on the ball of clay picks it up and turns to the others.

19   Silence.

Outcome

This short piece does not attempt to come to any sort of intellectual 'conclusion'. It has simply taken three things from a set of postcards and 'played' with them. But, by being guided by the postcards – and *trusting them* – the group was able to devise a sequence that had strong elements of theme and story.

We can see from this example how material that was initially offered as a 'getting to know each other' activity can provide a dynamic, inspirational source for dramatic creation. It is exactly this use of exchanged material that will continue to be encouraged throughout all the activities and the whole process.

Ask yourselves: How successful was your group in using someone else's ideas? How successful was the group in collaborating? How can you apply what you have learned to other work with your twin group?

Cross-reference

See Activity 56.

Activity 14 Dramatic boxes

In Activity 2 the groups exchanged boxes containing items that gave an impression of their environment: 'Our world'. The following activity is similar to Activity 8 in that it uses the material received as the basis for dramatic creation – the difference being that here we have actual objects – hopefully representing a range of the five senses – to work from and inspire us.

1 Open the box sent by your twin group. Examine the contents carefully. Think of them as a *gift* from your twin.

- This is an important marking-moment in your relationship with your twin group. Is there a ritual you can devise in opening the box?
- What do you think about your twin's objects?
- What surprises or shocks you?
- What inspires you?
- What did you not expect?
- What do the objects reveal about your twin company?
- What does your twin company want you to know about their world?

2 You are going to use the items to create a dramatic sequence. Once again, do not attempt to guess what the 'meaning' of the items is for your twin group. They are here to release your own creativity, in whatever manner you feel is appropriate. You may:

- create characters and scenes that the items suggest to you;
- create a poem or a song that the items inspire in you;
- build or create a community (real or imagined) that the items suggest to you;
- create a dance piece from the music you may have been sent;
- devise a ritual that incorporates all or some of the items.

3 Make a record of how you used the items from the box and send it to your twin.

4 Receive the record of how your twin used the items you sent to them.

Example 14.1

Here are examples of how three (random) items from a box could suggest a distinct character and a possible dramatic moment in their life.

1 The items are:
- a bar of scented soap
- a local newspaper
- a photo of a dead seagull, covered in oil.

The character and the moment: A reporter on a local newspaper. It is her birthday and she has just been given a box of scented soap as a gift. She is sent to investigate an oil-spillage at the beach. The sight of birds and sea life dead and dying on the shore upsets her greatly. She tears open the gift and attempts to clean a seagull's wings with it.

2 The items are:
- a poster from a Bollywood film
- some locally made sweets
- a train ticket.

The character and the moment: He wants to be a Bollywood film star. He is running away from home to make his fortune. He has stolen enough money for a one-way ticket to the city. It is a long journey and he sits on the train, with only a few sweets – made by his mother – to eat.

Example 14.2

Here is an example of an improvisational ritual created from a box of items received by a group in Brazil (Companhia Novos Novos) from a group based in the UK (Young Blood, Leicester). The items were:

- candles
- music
- the British flag
- food items – chocolate, crisps
- travel brochures
- a newspaper
- a small teddy bear
- a plastic ball.

A group of acquaintances enter an unknown space. The place is lit by candlelight. The air is scented by the candles. There is loud music playing, with a strong beat. There is a table in the centre of the space, covered by the British flag. There is food on the table. There are travel brochures lying on the floor around the table. On a shelf there is a newspaper and a small teddy bear.

- At first, people begin to interact with the objects and sounds individually. Gradually, the environment creates the desire to interact in twos, threes and in small groups.
- A plastic ball is taken to represent the globe. Some people start to play with the globe. Someone sits by a candle and reads the news to a teddy bear.
- Some of the group start to use 'made-up' language in response to what is being read from the newspaper. Others join them.
- Food is tasted and shared.
- Other forms of non-verbal communication develop: hand-clapping, dancing to the music.
- Gradually the group begins to collect in a large circle around the table, clapping and moving and repeating phrases of the made-up language.

Example 14.3

Try variations on the above:

- An empty space with one item only. Establish a group relationship to the item. Then bring another item and see how that affects the dynamic of the improvisation.
- Add furniture or props of your own into the work. How do more familiar items impact upon the unfamiliar?
- Work in a fully non-verbal way, creating a totally visual ritual.

Outcome

The activities that the items in the box can inspire may be as varied in style and scope as your imaginations allow. In Example 14.1, the randomly selected items provided the basis for a specific and 'socially real' character and situation. In Example 14.2 an abstract world was created. Each outcome was based upon *fully trusting* the materials being used and discovering how very different items might be linked together into some coherent form. Each example shows how a type of poetic or dramatic 'truth' may be achieved by placing what may – at first – seem impossibly 'unlinked' things together. A British flag, a plastic ball, a newspaper and a teddy bear etc. help create a type of group ritual that gives a sense of a strange, new and mysterious world. A bar of scented soap, a newspaper and a picture of an oil-covered seagull give life to a vivid character and a recognisable human reaction to a situation. In neither case is there a 'right or wrong' – just what seems truthful and appropriate.

Cross-reference

See Activities 53 and 54.

Activity 15 A dramatic item

Staying with the box, use single items to see how new thoughts and inspirations can evolve from the simplest thing.

1   In small groups, take a single item from the box. Discuss it. Ask questions about it – some of the following, and others that come to mind:
    - Material – what is it made of?
    - Function – what is it for?
    - Condition – what is its shape or form?
    - Use – what can I do with it?
    - Time – where has it come from, where is it going?

- People – who might be associated with it (in its making, use or disposal etc.)?
- What memories, experiences or images from your own lives does the item evoke?

2 Devise a way of showing the journey of the item. Think about the following:

- Many lives have been associated with this object. It has been on a journey (and now it is in your hands). What was that journey? What stories might be associated with it? What places might be associated with it?
- Using any form you wish (words, movement, dance), present the journey of the object.
- On its journey, the object may be given the ability to speak for itself.

Example 15.1

The object is a *Coke can that has been crushed flat*, sent by a group in India to a group in the UK. It is something that is familiar all over the world – and for that reason, little thought is given to it. But it has been sent as an essential item in a box from another place, so it has significance for whoever sent it. Thinking about the questions in the activity, what stories might it tell about its journey? Do the questions suggest areas of *research*? Here are some of the stories derived from this one simple object:

- It was made in a factory. One of the people in the factory had gone to work there because they had been driven off their small farm by a large landowner.

- The water needed to fill the can with its liquid came from fresh, natural sources. The result of this has meant that the local wells have run dry. A woman is walking many miles to draw water from a distant well.

- The can is transported (along with hundreds of others) to a distant city. The truck driver has been on the road for many months and has not seen his family in all that time.

- The can is for sale in a shop in the city. A woman looks at the can of Coke and dreams of being a top-flight model advertising the product on the television.

- A man in a business suit buys the can. He is going to an important meeting and decides he is going to need the 'extra energy' the product promises in order to impress his bosses. He sits on a bench and drinks hurriedly, then throws the can down.

- A young girl picks up the can. She takes it to her home in a poor part of the city, where the homes are made from discarded materials.

- The girl's father flattens the can, to add to the others that are going to patch up the roof of their home.
- A street theatre group arrives. One of the actors asks if he can use the can as a prop in the performance. He forgets to give it back.
- The crushed can is sent in a box, along with other items, to another theatre group.
- What might a similar journey of such an item be in the UK?

Outcome

The 'one item' activity tells us some important things about the use of all the materials sent by the twin group:

- Nothing is 'too insignificant' to be used creatively. If something has 'meaning' for the twin group, you should be able to discover your own meanings, from which dramatic situations and interesting characters can be developed.
- Research is invaluable. From this activity, we have seen how research into the production, consumption and uses of a specific object can spark off any number of human stories.

Cross-reference

See Activities 53 and 54.

Activity 16 Day stories

In Activity 3, the groups exchanged examples of 'a day in the lives' of their members. In this activity, that material will be used to develop scenes and characters. As with the other activities in this chapter, the groups are encouraged fully to engage with the material. The difference here is that individuals are beginning to reveal more of their lived lives, their daily experiences. However, the attempt is not *necessarily* simply to reproduce what the material is describing, but – once again – to allow it to inspire dramatic creation that has its own life. It is a question of *honouring the source material* but not being inhibited by it.

1   Take one of the 'day accounts' from your twin group. As a whole group or in small teams see what it suggest in terms of dramatic development.

2   Ask yourselves how the account of a day – or part or parts of a day – from another culture or community might 'translate' into the experience of your own culture or community. Is there a story that might emerge? (See Example 16.1.)

3   See if you can add to your twin's day story by introducing something of your own lives into it. Is there a story that might emerge? (See Example 16.2.)

4   Work in a style or manner that seems to have the most original creative scope: fully or partially verbal, non-verbal, imagistic, musical etc.

Example 16.1

A map of an area in Mumbai was made. Significant things that happen on a particular day were noted. A young street girl is accused of stealing a coin from a tourist. The tourist defends the girl, and she shows her around a part of the city. At the end of the day, the tourist buys some 'baby milk powder' – something she needs to feed her baby sister with.

Example 16.2

Someone in the UK is keeping an account of the times of day in Malaysia. She is thinking about a friend of hers who is visiting Malaysia. The day before her friend left, they quarrelled and parted on bad terms. She imagines what her friend might be doing at different times of the day. She makes up stories about her friend. The clock strikes midnight. She falls asleep. She dreams of her friend. Her friend enters her dream and tells her that she never wants to come home.

Activity 17 Food stories

In Activity 4, the groups exchanged a wide range of material related to food: its production, distribution and consumption; the symbolic and cultural references attached to it; the habits, customs and taboos that may be associated with it. As one of the basic necessities of life shared by every human being, food – and all its related aspects – provides a wealth of creative source material for a collaborative process.

   Here are some activities you may try. The first two use materials from Activity 4 – your own and those received from your twin. The third is a new exploration.

Part one – the cookery lesson

1   You will eventually be working in pairs – person A and person B.

2   Person A takes a recipe that was provided by someone from the twin group. They will need some time to study it – and perhaps do some private research. The object is to become something of an 'expert' on the subject – becoming familiar with the unfamiliar. The research could well include:

- finding out about food items that are unfamiliar;
- finding out about the history, culture and society of the region;
- learning words and phrases from the region.

3   There will now be an improvised scene: a cookery lesson. Person A will be 'the cook/instructor' and person B 'the helper/instructed'. Items of food, utensils etc. can be real or imagined. Keep the improvisation as simple – but as detailed – as possible. Resist any temptation to 'act' or to create characters. The focus should be strictly upon the task – the teaching of it and the learning of it.

4   Repeat the improvisation, but this time give person B a 'hidden agenda' – something that affects how he or she relates to the process, giving it a dramatic twist. Try for something that has to do with the subject matter of the task (the type of food, the culture the recipe comes from etc.). The focus will still be on the teaching/learning relationship, but will subtly affect the way in which person B behaves.

5   Exchange the results of your work with your twin group.

See Example 17.1.

Part two – sharing the food

1   Look at examples of mealtime habits, customs and manners – from your own material and from that of your twin.

2   Divide the group into small teams. Assign each team a particular set of habits etc.

3   Create an improvisation. In this, imagine that different groups of people – with their varying habits concerning food and its consumption – find themselves in the same place. Food is in short supply, and there is a need to share among the groups. Decide what the situation is. Do not force events with anything overly dramatic – allow things to evolve gradually:

- What reactions are there to unfamiliar foods?
- What responses are there to unfamiliar ways of eating?
- What things cause offence, arouse curiosity or give rise to dispute?
- Who takes initiatives, who withdraws from conflict, who looks for confrontation, who seeks to create harmony?
- What are the boundaries between the desire to hold on to the familiar and the need to embrace the unfamiliar?
- What new allegiances are formed?
- What old prejudices are aroused?

4   *Exchange* the results of your work with your twin group.

See Example 17.2.

Part three – different eating environments

If live theatre is 'human behaviour in action', then – as we have seen with the two activities above – all aspects of food (preparation, consumption, social engagement around it etc.) can be seen as 'performance'. The food is both actual and symbolic, and the potential for drama inhabits every aspect surrounding it. It is no coincidence that all forms of drama and stories worldwide feature family meals, feasts, banquets, fasting, starving, gluttony and famine etc. In a folk tale from Bengal, the god Bidatha dooms a poor Brahman to a particular fate: he is never allowed to eat to his heart's content, for when he has eaten half his rice, something always occurs to interrupt him. In Shakespeare's play *Titus Andronicus*, a parent is tricked by his enemy into eating a pie containing his own child!

In the previous two activities we have seen how the 'food for thought' material exchanged by the twin groups can provide – literally – 'fodder for drama'. Here we will see that the groups can further inspire each other by offering examples of different 'eating environments' from their own cultures.

As a group – or in small teams – visit environments in your own society or community where the 'food cultures' are different. Make a detailed record of what you experienced, what you learned, what you felt and what the different forms of human behaviour were. See how they suggest to you – and your twin group – opportunities for dramatic narratives.

See Example 17.3.

Example 17.1

The recipe could be for:

- a traditional Lancashire hotpot (stew);
- a traditional South Asian vegetarian meal.

The 'hidden agenda' could be:

- Person B has a prejudice against all things to do with English culture.
- Person B has a prejudice against vegetarianism.

Example 17.2

Three groups of people – from different communities – have been rounded up by the military. They have each managed to bring some food supplies with them. They are:

- a group that is strictly vegetarian;
- a group that practises religious fasting;
- a group that despises all forms of food that is not 'junk food'.

They find themselves sharing a guarded encampment. They do not know how long they will be there. Food is in short supply, and the need to share is becoming obvious. The scene is about the negotiations (power struggles, shifts in attitudes etc.) between the groups. The two unifying elements in the scene are (a) the 'micro' – the necessity to find ways of immediate survival; and (b) the 'macro' – the unseen presence of the guards.

Example 17.3

This extended example consists of extracts from a week-long workshop conducted by the Evam Youth Forum in India. It was called 'Feeding Performance', and its aim was to look at and experience the culture of food in different spaces with different people. In their own words, the young artists 'became involved in "doing" rather than "making" – shifting their focus from product to process, and also giving attention to everyday aspects of life, where both everything and nothing were important'.

Afternoon meal at a Gurdwara
Langar is the term used in the Sikh religion for free, vegetarian-only food served in a Gurdwara (Sikh temple, literal translation 'teacher's door'). Everyone sits as equals. Everyone is welcome to share the Langar, no-one is turned away. Each week, a family or several families volunteer to provide and prepare the Langar. All the preparation, the cooking and the washing up are also done by voluntary helpers.

How do men and women interact inside a religious space? I find it remarkable the way people are able to surrender themselves physically before a holy object. I realize that that physical experience is completely alien to me . . . What am I missing? That's what I want to know.

The food was splendid. Probably because it was my first time at a Langar, I found myself almost pathetically grateful to the people who were serving me. The others around me didn't seem to be thinking about it at all. They were there, they knew they were entitled to food, and were eating away . . . I did feel a resistance in me when I was served food with words like '*Wahe Guru!*'

(Ajay, from Evam Youth Forum)

The sight of women making chapattis has reminded me of my childhood days. It gave me a sense of doing something in a group with a common motive and no self-interest attached to it. The sense of being with so many people and eating with them, all of us sitting on mats, has overpowered the discomfort generated by the hot environment.

(Hyder, from Evam Youth Forum)

Afternoon meal at McDonalds

The second exercise in consumption was at a familiar place, which the participants attempted to look at with fresh eyes. It was the epitome of instant food, instant gratification ... this venue was placed right after a community meal rooted in tradition.

> The first few bites are good, but after that I get lost! This happens frequently when I eat fast food ... I start to enjoy what I'm eating, but soon I'm completely distracted from the food. I start talking or am lost in thinking quietly to myself. I completely forget to enjoy the food. It's eating mechanically after that ... the texture of the chicken cutlet inside the burger was smooth and uniform and it went in faster. I think that is what makes it difficult to savour the taste for too long.
>
> (Soumya, from Evam Youth Forum)

> The attractive blown-up photographs of close-ups of the freshest of natural vegetables went hand in hand with the hackneyed, processed foods that one consumes there. The whole event felt like a concentrated, full-speed ride that was over before we knew it. It was a scary after-thought that maybe fast food was not designed to match our fast-paced metropolitan life, but to rather induce it.
>
> (Sujay, from Evam Youth Forum)

Food at households

On the following days, the participants were engaged in much more than the act of consumption. They were in involved the 'performing food cycle' – provisioning, preparing, serving, consuming and disposing. Everything from buying the vegetables to putting the dishes back in racks after washing.

> Sujay and I went to the market together to buy some vegetables and meat ... It was a place screaming with life – throbbing with sounds of the sharpening of the butcher's knife, the fluttering of the chickens, the squabbling and haggling over prices, the tossing of weights into primitive scales and so on ... Every sense was overwhelmed there. My eyes feasted on blood red tomatoes, grasshopper green peas and wine hued blood congealing on the table tops ... The smells get nearly intoxicating.
>
> One of the high points was at Mrs Das's house. We were handling the raw, soft and pink chicken with all our hands in it together, to marinate it. I've never had such an experience with carnality in a group together, it felt like we were all physically connected through the chicken. Music was also an important part of the food ritual here. This was a household of musicians – Namit and his mother are singers. She would take a break from the cooking to simply sit in the living room and sing for five minutes while he played the harmonium. Music and story-telling became an integral part of the cooking and eating.
>
> (Rachel, from Evam Youth Forum)

The kind of constraints one experienced in organizing and adjusting oneself spatially amidst the chaos in a narrow, strip-like kitchen could be compared to a workshop exercise on the floor where spatial limitations are forced upon a performer in order to induce a heightened sense of movement.

(Sujay, from Evam Youth Forum)

Eating alone

On the last day, participants went by themselves to a public space such as a stall by the beach or food courts at malls, to experience eating amid people by oneself.

Since I had no group or circle to close myself in, I found myself much more open to people, much more observant of my surroundings, watching and sometimes overhearing other groups intently. At the same time I also felt a little insecure, because I had no familiar circle to close myself in . . . it felt like time was moving faster outside me, while within me it was progressing in some sort of slow motion.

(Rachel, from Evam Youth Forum)

Outcome

We have seen that the subject matter of 'food' extends much further than exchanging aspects of cultural similarities and differences. All of its aspects – from the gathering or the buying, through the preparation and eating, to the clearing up – have performative aspects. The thoughts, reflections, memories and insights all the activities invite produce rich material for drama.

Activity 18 Scenes from phrases

In Activity 5, the groups exchanged lists of completed phrases. You are going to create a scene, dialogue or monologue from phrases your twin group has sent you.

Part one – an 'I love' dramatic scene

1   Look at the list of 'I love . . .' phrases your twin has sent you.
2   Decide on a situation where a group has to make a *choice*. The list of phrases may provide a clue as to what the situation may be. It could be 'high intensity' (such as breaking out of a prison) or 'low intensity' (such as choosing teams for a game). Whatever the situation is, character conflict, shifts in allegiance etc. will emerge.

3 There may be a range of outcomes to the scene:
   - Everyone willingly makes the same decision.
   - Everyone makes the same decision, but with different levels of agreement.
   - Some people make their own decisions.
4 The scene can be improvised and – if appropriate – written up later.
5 Everyone in the group is allocated one of the phrases. Give everyone a few moments to think about the phrase and see what clue it gives as to the character they will be playing.
6 The first time that anyone speaks in the scene, they must include somewhere in their speech their phrase. They can return to the phrase (or parts of it) at other times in the scene if they wish.
7 The focus of the improvisation is therefore on:
   - the choice that the group has to make;
   - the character that the phrase suggests to each performer.

See Example 18.1.

Part two – an 'I wish' character dialogue

1 Work in pairs. You are going to create (improvise or write) a dialogue between two people.
2 Look at the list of 'I wish . . .' phrases from your twin group. See what clues the phrases give as to the situation: where the two people are, what they are doing etc. Try and be as imaginative as possible here – two people sitting in a room can be interesting, but two people sitting up a tree could be more interesting dramatically.
3 Each person takes alternate phrases. Decide what clues your phrases give for the type of character you will be playing.
4 Do not worry if there is no dramatic outcome to the scene – think of this as an opportunity to explore 'character'.
5 Each time one of the characters speaks they must include one of their phrases. All the phrases must be used. They can be used more than once if appropriate to the scene.

See Example 18.2.

Part three – an 'I don't understand' monologue

Another way of using the completed phrases is to use them to develop individual monologues.

1 Work individually. Look at the list of 'I don't understand . . .' phrases sent by your twin group.

2   The task is to link the phrases into one long speech. Include all the phrases, in the order that they appear. They will be the 'spine' of the monologue, and you will weave them together with your own words.

3   The trick here is *not to plan*: don't attempt to think of a character or a situation, just start with the first phrase, see what words follow and find your way to the next phrase. Do not worry if you feel it is not 'making sense' – just have fun allowing the phrases to guide you.

See Example 18.3.

Example 18.1

The scene is developed from the list of 'I love . . .' phrases in Example 5.1.
    The situation suggested from the phrases: a group is on holiday together. They have one means of transport and they have to decide what to do today. The improvisation begins like this:

A: Because I love all my ex girlfriends I want to drive to the beach and take photographs to send to them all.

B: Can't we go to the next big town? There's a big demonstration going on and I love politics when they happen on the streets.

A: You wouldn't catch any of my ex girlfriends having anything to do with politics.

B: My vote is the beach. I love the knowledge that everyone is equal when they are swimming in the water.

C: No, no . . . it's too hot on the beach, let's go up to the mountains . . . there's snow and ice and I love the winter weather.

D: I'm not going anywhere, the World Match is on the television and I love Manchester United football club.

E: But that is so selfish, you're the only driver. I love all who can be loved, but you don't deserve my affection if that is your attitude.

A: None of my ex girlfriends would like him, either.

Etc.

Example 18.2

The dialogue is developed from the list of 'I wish . . .' phrases in Example 5.1.
    The situation: two people are standing in the wings waiting to go on for a performance of a school play.

A: I'm so nervous, I'm always like this before I go onstage. I wish it were the school holidays and this was all over.

B: I wish my grandmother was still alive, she always loved to see me acting.

A: I've forgotten all my lines . . . I'll make a fool of myself. Oh, I wish it would rain so hard the roof would start leaking and the whole thing got cancelled.

B: No, no . . . we'll be a big hit, we'll be discovered and go to Bollywood . . . I wish I could see into the future . . .

A: You can keep Bollywood or Hollywood or . . . I just wish I had a pet dog and lived all alone where no-one could ever find me.

Etc.

Example 18.3

This example will use 'I don't understand . . .' phrases from Activity 5.

> I do not understand electronics. I am sure they have their uses, but when they are used to control people I worry a lot. Why do we need to be controlled? I do not understand the severe security in front of the American Embassy. Do they think we are such a threat . . . is that all we are to them? I do not understand narrow-minded people, I really don't. The other day a friend started to talk about 'fame' as if that is all there is to life. She said 'I don't understand why I'm not a superstar in Hollywood', and asked me to help her write a list of all the things that would make her a star. I said, 'I don't understand the point of this exercise' . . . Etc.

Outcome

The activity and its examples show how the results of a simple 'getting to know you' exchange of thoughts and phrases can begin to provide material for scenes, dialogues and monologues. Characters, situations and dramatic events start to emerge – all possible avenues that the group may wish to go down in creating their play. A true collaborative process is beginning to emerge.

Cross-reference

See Activity 58.

Activity 19 Dramatic questions

In Activity 6, the groups exchanged lists of questions. The value of 'asking questions' was considered. As we will see later on, all plays have large, universal questions at their heart – things that cannot be answered with a simple 'yes' or 'no', but that address in complex ways the nature and experience of being human.

For the moment, it is useful to continue the encouragement of the 'questioning muscle' – exploring a thought or an idea through constant questions (keeping things 'open') and resisting the urge to give an answer or an opinion ('closing off'). In this activity, we will see how such work can provide even more material and inspiration for the collaborative process.

Part one – questions from questions

1   Look at the lists of questions your twin group sent you.

2   Select *one* question from one of the lists. This is the *governing question*.

3   Ask three questions that are prompted by the governing question.

4   Ask three more questions for each of the three subsequent questions.

5   Continue this process for as long as the questions keep coming. By the end you will have a 'cascade' of questions, all flowing from the original governing question.

6   Try not to think what the answers to the questions might be. Some of the questions may be big, 'universal' ones, others may be quite specific and personal ones. Don't worry if the questions do not seem to 'make sense' – or indeed seem ridiculous or unimportant. The main thing is to frame *all your thoughts as questions* and see how many you can ask.

7   *Exchange* the results of the activity with your twin.

See Example 19.1.

Part two – questions into scenes

You are going to use some of the questions from one of the 'cascades' sent by your twin as the basis for an improvisation.

1   Look at one of the 'cascades' of questions received from your twin group.

2   The *governing question* will be the title (or focus) of the scene.

3   Take three of the subsequent questions from the list.

4   Work in groups of three. Each person is allocated one of the questions. The question is a clue to the *type* of person they might be – some quality of character, personality, intellect etc. that is somehow essential to them.

5   Spend a few moments thinking about what the question you have been allocated might suggest.

6   Decide on a situation – place, event or moment in time – that the three characters inhabit.

7   Explore the characters through an improvisation (five to ten minutes maybe). Do not think ahead too much, nor plan for a particular dramatic outcome. The object of the improvisation is to *explore character* rather than strive for a 'closing moment'.

8   Try different sets of questions and repeat the process.

9   Write up the improvisation. Exchange the results with your twin.

See Example 19.2.

Example 19.1

The question is from the 'questions about myself' category in Activity 6.

1   *Governing question*: Why do I always have such strong opinions about everything?

2   Subsequent questions prompted by the governing question:
   •   What is a strong opinion?
   •   Where do strong opinions come from?
   •   Is 'something' better than 'everything?'

3   Questions prompted by the three subsequent questions:

   What is a strong opinion?
   •   What is strength?
   •   What makes an opinion strong?
   •   Do I care what you think?

   Where do strong opinions come from?
   •   What did I learn from my parents?
   •   Do the newspapers lie?
   •   What is a Big Idea?

   Is 'something' better than 'everything'?
   •   Should I be like a poem or a hammer?
   •   Is it best to keep my mouth shut?
   •   Do dead people fill my head with their thoughts?

4   Questions prompted by the questions:

   What is strength?
   •   Will the meek inherit the earth?
   •   Will I win the race tomorrow?
   •   Is the pen mightier than the sword?

   What makes an opinion strong? (Add your own examples.)

   Do I care what you think? (Add your own examples.)

Example 19.2

1   The *governing question*: Why do I always have such strong opinions about everything?

2   The three subsequent questions (as a basis for 'character type'):

  •   (Character A) What is strength?
  •   (Character B) Do newspapers lie?
  •   (Character C) Will I win the race tomorrow?

3   Notes about the characters suggested by the question that is somehow central to the type of person they are:

  •   *What is strength?* (Character A) This person is unsure of herself. She has strong opinions, but can be easily swayed by the opinions of others. She is a bit of a loner.
  •   *Do newspapers lie?* (Character B) This person is obsessed with 'the news'. He believes everything he reads and is very opinionated. He loves the gossip columns.
  •   *Will I win the race tomorrow?* (Character C) This person trains every day, to the point of exhaustion. She won't take the advice that 'there is more to life than winning'.

4   Possible situations (and dramatic moments) for an improvised scene between the three characters:

  •   A park bench: character A listens to characters B and C talking about world events. She disagrees with them, but struggles to find a way to make her own thoughts known.
  •   A newspaper office, where the big news just coming in is a scandal about drug taking by famous athletes: character B sees this as his chance to become a top reporter. Characters A and C have different attitudes.
  •   The day before a marathon race: character C will be taking part and is determined to win. Characters A and B have different attitudes on the notion of 'winning'.

Outcome

From one single *governing question*, we already have a long list of subsequent questions. If the example had continued, there would have been many more.

Why do I always have such strong opinions about everything?

  •   What is a strong opinion?
  •   Where do strong opinions come from?
  •   Is 'something' better than 'everything'?
  •   What is strength?
  •   What makes an opinion strong?
  •   Do I care what you think?
  •   What did I learn from my parents?

- Do the newspapers lie?
- What is a Big Idea?
- Is a strong opinion like a hammer?
- Is it best to keep my mouth shut?
- Do dead people fill my head with their thoughts?
- Will the meek inherit the earth?
- Will I win the race tomorrow?
- Is the pen mightier than the sword?

By resisting the urge to 'give answers', a great range of thoughts, ideas and images have flowed from that one first question. By avoiding 'closure' there has been a constant 'opening out', and all of this provides rich, creative source material for the work you are doing.

- From what might seem – at first – a random selection of questions, we have seen how they can provide the basis for dramatic narratives, the creation of characters and the exploration of themes and subject matters. As ever, the material sent by 'the twin' is *never* just 'information': it is rich source material that can inspire us and encourage our own creativity.

Cross-reference

See Activities 37–38 and 53.

Activity 20 Photograph stories

We are discovering, through the creative-twinning process, that 'your story' can become 'my story' can become 'our story'. In this activity, you are going to provide your twin group with a story that is purely visual. It will be a linear progression of events that is not 'explained' by language. Your twin group will receive your visual story and retell it – through the addition of language – in a manner that seems truthful to them.

1   Decide on an activity that includes everyone in the group. It should be one in which a progression of things 'happen'. It can take place anywhere and it should be something that is familiar to your lives – a party, a sporting event, an outing, a meal or a lesson in a classroom, for example. Try for something that is quite ordinary and daily. Try and avoid anything that is 'over-dramatic' (no murders or aliens from outer space arriving etc.).

2   The time frame should be linear (no sudden shifts into the past or the future). It should be a relatively simple story of a group of people engaging in an activity.

3   Decide what the key moments are in this story:
    • When do conflicts arise?
    • How do different people react to the progression of events?
    • How are conflicts resolved?
    • What are the outcomes?

4   Go for about ten to twelve 'key moments'. Take a photograph of each of these moments. Number the images.

5   *Send* the numbered images to your twin group. Do not explain the story – allow the story to speak for itself.

6   *Receive* the numbered images from your twin group. Ask yourselves:
    • What is happening here?
    • Who is doing what and why are they doing it?
    • Who is saying what?

7   Supply the dialogue to the sequence of pictures you have been given. You can do this through improvisation and/or writing. It might be that you create a cartoon-strip sequence, by adding speech bubbles. Avoid trying to guess at what your twin group was saying – what their story was – and see if you can allow the images to inspire you to create your own story out of what you have received.

8   Use your own first language in adding the words to the images, or a variety of languages (or a made-up language if that seems appropriate).

9   *Send* the results to your twin group. Include translation if you wish.

Example 20.1

1   A group in the UK is engaged in the activity of learning how to rock climb.

2   A group in India is engaged in the activity of cooking a meal.

3   A group in the UK is engaged in the activity of making masks for a theatre performance.

4   A group in Brazil is engaged in the activity of making placards and banners for a public demonstration.

Outcome

The 'original story' – the one that was presented in photographic images – has been translated (possibly literally) though the imaginations of people from another culture.

As ever, there is no 'right or wrong' here – it is simply another manifestation of how the creative impulse of one group of people can inspire that of another group. How 'our story' becomes 'their story' becomes *our stories*.

Activity 21 Active memories

In this activity, we will look at how memories – individual and collective – can be shared and developed as the basis for stories.

Theatre is an act of collective remembering. The telling or retelling of story and the receiving of that story are part of our connection with the past and our shared journeys into the future. In this sense, the audience (even in the most conventional type of auditorium) is not a passive entity: there are the 'communicators' (the actors) and the 'communicants' (the audience). Indeed, the religious roots of many forms of theatre around the world bear this out – where everyone is involved in the ritualistic re-enactment of shared memories, beliefs and traditions. From the Greek classical tragedies, to the English 'mystery plays' (based on the Bible), to the Ramayana myths, there is the thread of re-enactment of the symbolic underpinning of cultures.

In the making of 'new theatre' we are – consciously or unconsciously – placing ourselves in the tradition of a craft that has, at its heart, the task (some would say duty) of renewing our collective memory. The new narratives we make and their symbolic representation in public performance bring to that tradition the experience of 'the now'.

In the creative exchange of artists from different cultures, the new theatre that is being made plays a vital role in a renewal of theatre – a theatre that reflects the ever-increasing ways in which our lives on this planet are interdependent. The exchange of memory between the participants is a rich source of material for the narratives we are making.

1   Record memories:
    •   *Personal memory*: Working individually, record a memory that has significance in your own life, something that helped shaped you as a person.
    •   *Local shared memories*: Working in small groups, record a memory of something that everyone in your own community would share, an event of some significance.
    •   *Global shared memories*: Working in small groups, record the memory of an event most or many people in the world would recognise.
    See Example 21.1.
2   *Exchange* the memories with your twin group.
3   Work in small groups. Devise ways of fusing the memories you have received with your own memories. Don't feel you need to use everything – select what appeals to you. Use different methods:
    •   through conventional character dialogue or monologue;
    •   through poems or songs;
    •   through dance or movement;
    •   through ritual.
    See Example 21.2.
4   *Exchange* the results with your twin group.

Example 21.1

1   *Personal memory*:

> It was my first trip out of this continent, in the Van Gogh Museum in Amsterdam. Time completely stopped for me, and I found myself completely transported. I still find it odd to say this, but for the first time in my life I was not thinking. No language was running in my head, decoding what I was seeing, no sentences, no lines, no words. I just stared. It was the most wonderful feeling I've ever felt, a warm ebullience; a freedom I'd never felt before, a maddening exhilarating rush.
>
> (Naren, from Evam Youth Forum, India)

> I was eight years old. I had in my hand a piece of cake. The child was poor. She saw the cake. I saw the look in her eyes. I recognized her sadness. I did not eat the cake. I did not give it to her.
>
> (Company member, The Studio Theatre, Syria)

2   *Local memory*:

Examples of local memories from the UK include:

*   'A tidal surge along the coast, and everyone putting sandbags against their front doors';
*   'When the city football team won the cup final';
*   'The day when the town had its first Gay Festival'.

3   *Global memory*:

Examples of global memories include:

*   'The news that Nelson Mandela had been freed from prison, and the words he spoke about wanting a South Africa in which everyone is equal';
*   'Seeing the Twin Towers burning on the television, and thinking that it was a Hollywood movie';
*   'The tsunami happening in Asia and devastating the coast'.

Example 21.2

An example of how a personal, a local and a global memory inspired a three-part dramatic sequence, using image, movement and one key word:

1   Someone is in an art gallery, looking at a painting by Van Gogh. The crows in the picture come alive and take flight.

2   The crows circle. They call out. The person remains silent. The crows sound as if they are chanting the word 'Freedom'.

3   Another person – of the same gender as the first – enters. The two people kiss.

Outcome

The activity has shown how:

- 'memory' can be personal and public, private and shared;
- one memory can activate other memories;
- memory is 'active' – it is the process of making sense of things that have happened;
- 'memory' can provide a rich source for dramatic invention – bringing together things that do not initially seem to 'belong' together (what have crows in a picture by Van Gogh, Nelson Mandela and two people of the same gender kissing have to do with each other?).

Cross-reference

See Activities 30 and 58.

Activity 22 Rituals

Ritual. The prescribed or established form of a religious or other ceremony. An activity that preserves the memory and traditions of a community or group.

The use of 'ritual' – as a form of theatrical presentation – has been noted at several points along the way so far. It will be referred to throughout the book and in many of the activities offered. In this activity, you will be creating your own rituals – to be shared with your twin group and developed together – New Rituals.

In many cultures, the collective ceremony of the ritual has its roots in religion – whether the established major world religions of today, the ceremonies in ancient Greece or Rome related to the gods and goddesses, or specific tribal ceremonies from around the world. They are often related to the marking of special events in the life of the community or the individual:

- birth, marriage, death;
- wars, victories, acts of remembrance;
- 'rites of passage' – from one life stage to another;
- thanksgivings – for the benefits of nature, salvation from natural disaster;
- the establishment of leaders – coronations, elections.

Ritual is therefore very much bound up with memory – the collective and the individual; the formal (symbolic) marking of an event that has significance, linking the past and the future with the present.

1   Think about your own culture or community and the rituals that are in use today. They can be large-scale and 'national', highly formal or relatively informal, derived from ancient practices or more contemporary experiences. List as many of these as you can (see Example 22.1).

2   *Exchange* these with your twin.

3   Create a new ritual that is specific to your group. Attempt to make something that:
    •   is related to the work you are doing together;
    •   involves everyone;
    •   is both symbolic and practical.

4   *Exchange* these with your twin (see Example 22.2).

5   Using the exchanged work, create a ritual that contains elements of your own ritual and those of your twin's (see Example 22.3).

Example 22.1

Here are some examples of rituals that exist in the UK today:

•   national 'marking events' – the coronation or the burial of a monarch, the annual Remembrance Day Service for the war dead, the election of a Prime Minister;

•   ritual ceremonies, events or observances associated with the different major religions – Easter, Ramadan, Eid;

•   the celebration of victories – the awarding of trophies to a football team, the 'victory parade' of sports competitors;

•   rediscovered ancient rituals related to nature – the Druids celebrating the summer solstice;

•   the exchange or giving of gifts at important moments in someone's life – birthdays, marriages;

•   communal events that derive from a past history that may have been forgotten, but that still lives on in a symbolic form – Bonfire Night (the burning of a 'guy' on a large fire (accompanied by fireworks), which has its roots in the history of Guido Faukes, a seventeenth century Catholic who was part of a plot to blow up the Protestant King of England);

•   ritual meal ceremonies: the Thanksgiving dinners in North America are a ritual that remembers the gift of food and sustenance that the New World offered the original European settlers and colonisers of that past.

Example 22.2

1   The Studio Theatre in Damascus, Syria, had a very simple ritual related to the space they were working in. They called it 'the sacred space' – the

defined area of floor on which the creative activities took place. Before stepping into this space, the simple ritual activity consisted of the removal of all footwear – the sacred space was the place of bare feet, where the connection between the 'earth' (the ground beneath the feet) and the imagination was not contaminated by the dust of the outside world.

2   A group in the UK began each day's session by sitting in a circle. Each member of the group would bring a small object or image that had significance for them. They would speak about this briefly. The objects and images were placed in a 'shrine' before the work began.

3   At the end of the week's work, each member of a group in the UK would write (or draw) something that was a very private expression of what they had felt or experienced during the week. They could express positive or negative feelings or thoughts. These were not shared by anyone. The group would then process to an outside area, where they stood in a circle around a small fire. The sheets of paper were burned on the fire. The group stood in a circle and watched the smoke ascend. This was all done in silence.

Example 22.3

Here is an example of how elements from two different rituals can provide the inspiration for a third one:

1   Each member of the group writes a single word on a piece of paper. The word expresses a feeling they have had during a working session.

2   A 'sacred space' is marked out on the floor.

3   In bare feet, each member of the group in turn enters the space and places the word on the floor. As they place the word, they speak it. The group repeats the word.

4   The start of the next session begins with the words being turned into a song.

Outcome

•   On a very practical level, a ritual can help to prepare a group for the work in hand. The creation of a 'sacred space' gives a dynamic meaning to the place that the work is taking place in – creating a symbolic gesture that focusses the energy of the group onto that space. (One group I worked with started each day by 'ritualistically' leaving all their coats, bags etc. outside the room they were working in – literally and symbolically shedding the 'daily' world before entering the creative one.)

- The repetition of the ritual can enhance the sense of the collective spirit in a group – an agreed symbolic activity that gives an essence of the purpose and the shared history of the group.

- Established rituals we know or observe today – coronations, victory parades, thanksgivings etc – have all adapted from rituals of the past. The Christian Christmas and Easter rituals have their roots in the rituals of pre-Christian times. In creating our own New Rituals, we can also adapt and develop them through a creative exchange with other cultures we are working with.

Activity 23 Hidden histories

Many of the activities so far have created material that draws upon the lives and experiences of group members – personal histories, daily routines, thoughts, feelings etc. In this activity, groups will be looking at aspects of their world – country, community, region etc. – that are often overlooked or forgotten. So this activity starts with a process of 'retrieval' – researching into the past or recent histories of 'place': those things that do not always get into the 'official histories'.

History is indeed in the hands of those who write it (often the 'winners', the powerful or the orthodox establishment). After World War II, American historians had a large hand in the creation of a new history curriculum for that part of Germany (West Germany) that was now part of the Western Alliance. West Germany – so recently 'the enemy', but now defeated – was to be an ally of the USA against Russia, which was in occupation of East Germany. It was therefore in the interests of the USA (and her allies) to create a situation in which the West Germans no longer felt burdened by, or guilty for, their recent past – the fascist regime of Adolf Hitler. Consequently, the history books that young people in West Germany studied did not dwell upon those recent events – indeed the curriculum, by side-stepping those events, made it seem as if they were almost inconsequential. I remember, in the early 1960s, going on an exchange visit to West Germany and staying with a German family. When a conversation arose between myself and the son of the house, he spoke of 'in the time of the Nazis', as if it were some dim and distant past. It seemed to me that he was remembering that time in the way I remembered the Viking invasions of Britain fifteen hundred years ago.

There has been a painful retrieval of memory in Germany more recently – in West Germany of the complicity of the population in the Holocaust, and in East Germany of the collusion with the communist secret police (the Stasi). Other examples of retrieval of 'hidden histories' are found around the world. In the UK there is an annual Black History month, during which the ongoing rediscovery of the contribution of black people to the country is given prominence. The month celebrates the contribution that black people have made to the history, culture and economy of the UK. Lesbian and gay communities have rediscovered the ways in which people of differing sexuality have similarly contributed to the world. Native populations have refound traditions, histories and stories that conquest, slavery and 'official history' have buried or distorted. In small but significant ways, local history initiatives have revealed a past that is not just about kings, queens and the lords of the manor.

In this activity, the retrieval of history can be from any perspective or angle that is appropriate or interesting to the group: large discoveries about the nation or small ones about the locality.

Part one – interesting histories past and present

1   *Research* the histories, using whatever methods are appropriate:
    - libraries, newspapers, the internet;
    - live interviews with older citizens, family members, neighbours;
    - tombstones, monuments, buildings;
    - myths, local tales;
    - something about your immediate world – the seemingly familiar and ordinary – that conceals facts and stories that are astonishing, surprising or extraordinary.

    See Example 23.1.
2   Receive the hidden histories your twin group has sent you.
3   Select some of them and turn them into a dramatic sequence – an improvisation, a series of images, a movement piece etc.
4   Look at your own hidden histories and turn some of them into a dramatic sequence.

See Example 23.2.

Part two – a recent history that needs to be told

1   See if there is a true, human story from the recent past of your community that needs to be told – one that perhaps would not find its way into the media, and certainly one that your twin group would not know about. This may be a story developed from one of those you discovered in Part one of this activity – one that you feel deserves to be told at length because it carries a particular emotional weight, or has a strong dramatic theme and a subject matter of importance.
2   Try and make the story as full and as detailed as possible.
    See Example 23.3.
3   If you receive such a story from your twin, see if there is a way in which – without being unfaithful to the original – you can make a dramatic intervention into it (through a new character or a parallel story perhaps) that connects it with your own community or culture.

See Example 23.4.

Example 23.1

Here are some examples of hidden histories discovered by groups in the UK. They range from the tragic to the celebratory, the comic to the instructive, the local to the national:

- A gravestone in the town of Brighton. It is of Pheobe Hessell. She was born in London in 1745. As a young woman she dressed as a man and passed herself off as one. As such she joined the navy as a sailor, fought bravely in a sea battle and was given a medal for her (his) services. She lived to be 108.

- In the north of England in the early twentieth century, Lancashire cotton-mill workers met and welcomed Mahatma Gandhi. They listened to what he had to say about the unjust trade agreements imposed on India by the British government and went on strike to support Gandhi when he asked Indians to boycott cotton made in Britain.

- An ancient law, still on the statute books, makes it illegal to cross-dress within a mile of the City of Westminster (central London). So – officially – men can't wear dresses and women can't wear suits within a mile of Parliament.

- An ancient law states that it is illegal in the whole of England to eat mince pies (a small pie filled with fruit) on 25 December.

- An ancient law states that it is illegal for a Member of Parliament to enter the House of Commons wearing a full suit of armour.

- A woman called Mother Shipton was born in a cave in England in 1488. She wrote a book of prophecies, including one that could be predicting the motor car:

    Carriages without horses shall go
    And accidents fill the world with woe . . .

- One of the first records of a black person to come to Britain was a general (probably of North African origin) with the Roman army. He is known to have guarded Hadrian's Wall (the wall the Romans built to keep the Scots from invading).

- An antique-furniture store is called The Forge. The building was once a place where local farmers took their horses to be shod with iron horse-shoes. The fireplace where the metal was smelted is still there – occupied now by expensive oak furniture.

- As the story goes, the hill just outside London called Blackheath was the place where thousands of people were buried when the plague came to the city. The local myth is that 'the Plague is still down there' and will one day work its way back up to the surface.

- An arts and community centre in London has a large hall that was built in the eighteenth century. Around the top of the hall are balconies.

The building was originally a slave market. The people who went there to buy the slaves viewed the people they were buying from the balconies.

- Clapham Junction is a railway station in London. In 1895 the Irish playwright Oscar Wilde was arrested, tried and convicted under a law that made homosexuality illegal. Handcuffed and in prison clothing, he was taken to prison by his guards. But on the way he was forced to stand on the platform at Clapham Junction for two hours, where people were allowed to mock him and spit at him.

- The story goes that Boudicca – the warrior leader of an ancient British tribe who rebelled against the invading Romans – is buried under what is now a platform of one of London's main railway stations (Kings Cross).

- A German pilot during World War II, flying home from a bombing raid on London, dropped his remaining bombs on a seaside town, killing many people. In the 1970s, he returned to the town, and there was a moment of reconciliation between him and families who had suffered.

- A 'traditional' English dish is 'fish and chips'. But the meal – fish fried in rich batter and chips, also fried – was introduced into the English diet by Jewish immigrants.

- In the middle of the twentieth century, an English priest was denounced for indecent behaviour. He left the Church and eventually became a lion tamer in a seaside zoo. One day a lion ate him.

- A poet (Edward Carpenter) lived in the north of England in the late nineteenth century. At a time when homosexuality was punished by law, he had a succession of working-class male lovers – all called George!

Here is an example of the 'hidden history' of something from the daily, contemporary world – something that seems ordinary, but that conceals facts and figures that are quite extraordinary (and in some cases quite alarming). This comes from the group Chickenshed, London. The group called this hidden history 'Disgusting Statistics'.

During Autumn of 2000, a team of scientists at the Department of Forensics, University College London, removed a row of passenger seats from a Central Line tube carriage for analysis into cleanliness. Despite London Underground's claim that their trains are cleaned on a regular basis, the scientists made some alarming discoveries.

On the surface of the seats the following were found:

- four types of hair sample (human, mouse, rat, dog);
- seven types of insect (mostly fleas, mostly alive);
- vomit originating from at least nine separate people;

- human urine originating from at least four separate people;
- human excrement;
- rodent excrement;
- human semen.

When the seats were taken apart the following were found:

- the remains of six mice;
- the remains of two large rats;
- one previously unknown fungus.

Example 23.2

Here are some examples of ways that 'hidden histories' may be used as the basis for dramatic sequences. The style of presentation may vary – straight scene, as an opera, a song sequence, a stylised movement piece, a soap opera etc. Different ways of exploring one story might be tried.

- A man who is 108 years old has died. He is known to have been a brave sailor and received a medal for his service in battle. As the body is being prepared for burial it is discovered to be that of a woman.
- The great-granddaughter of an English cotton-mill worker visits India. She meets the great-grandson of an Indian worker who was involved in the boycott of English cotton organised by Gandhi.
- An Italian passenger on a platform at Kings Cross railway station meets the ghost of Boudicca. She thinks he is a Roman invader.
- A Jewish immigrant cooks a meal of fish with chips for his English neighbour. The neighbour steals the recipe and makes a fortune.
- A modern-day family is put on trial for eating mince pies on 25 December.

The 'Disgusting Statistics' hidden history from Chickenshed also provides possible material for dramatic scenes or sequences. How mice, rats and various human bodily fluids come to be present on and in the passenger seats of an underground train suggests a range of gruesome, comic or disturbing scenarios. The reader is left to her or his imagination here.

Example 23.3

This is a story from South Africa. It comes from the relatively recent past of the country, before the apartheid system was abolished. It is an example of a 'small story' with a large theme and an important subject matter, containing complex human dilemmas and several dramatic outcomes. It also tells us something about the nature of art and the potential it has for changing lives.

During the time of apartheid, a young black South African man was involved in political protest. For his troubles, he spent much of his adolescence in prison. As well as being a political activist he was also a poet, and while in prison he continued to write poetry.

One day, one of the prison warders – white, as were all the warders (the prisoners were all black) – came up to the young man and said 'You're the one who writes poems, eh?'. 'Yes', said the young man, 'I do write poems'. It turned out that the warder had a girlfriend, and it was soon to be her birthday. He wanted to send her, as a special gift, a love poem. 'But', he said to the young prisoner, 'I'm no good at that sort of thing. Will you write a poem for me and I will tell my girlfriend I made it for her?'

So the young black prisoner wrote a love poem for the girlfriend of the white warder whose job it was to keep him in captivity. Soon, word of this got around to all the other prison warders. They began asking the young man to write poems for them – for their mothers and their sweethearts, for anniversaries and birthdays.

The young man eventually found himself out of prison. One day he was walking along the street and saw the warder who had originally asked him to write the love poem for his girlfriend. The two men recognised each other and spoke. 'Are you still keeping people in prison?' said the young man. 'No', said the other, 'I stopped doing that'. 'Why was that?' asked the young man.

The reply he received was this. 'Well, I got to thinking. I was earning my living by keeping someone who wrote poetry locked up. It just didn't seem right. So I stopped.'

Example 23.4

The story of the young black poet and the white prison warder in South Africa was given to some young actors in the UK. This is how they developed it:

1   The basic outline of the story was kept as it was. The group decided to create, through improvisation, a fictional drama that was adjacent to the central story.

2   A new character in the story – the white warder's girlfriend – was developed. She became a young white woman from the UK who was spending her gap year in South Africa.

3   Through a succession of scenes, the meeting between the young white UK woman and the white South African man was explored. The man – discovering that the young woman held what he regarded as 'liberal' views on race issues – did not reveal what he did for a living. Eventually – just before she was to return to the UK after her birthday – he gives her a card with a love poem in it. He tells her he wrote it himself. He is hoping that it will impress her so much that she won't go back to the UK.

4   The young woman reads the poem out loud. She is moved and touched by it. But even so, she tells the man that she won't be staying in South Africa. She tells him that – even though they'll probably never meet again – she will always treasure the poem.

5   The man is disappointed and angry. But he remembers her words about the beauty of the poem. He thinks about the young black man who wrote it. He thinks about the fact that he lied to the young woman about the work he did. He realises that he can no longer live with himself as long as he earns his living by keeping people locked up.

Outcome

Whatever 'hidden histories' the groups send each other, they will all of them have given unique and original insights into the world of the twin. They will have:

*   broadened the knowledge of, and interest in, a new community or culture;
*   provided a rich source of material for the dramatic developments, some of which may find their way into the final plays.

With the extended use of the South African story in Example 23.3, we have seen how, by adding a 'fictionalised' element to a story, we can remain truthful to it and, at the same time, bring in an experience from our own culture.

Activity 24 Inspirational topics

This activity is somewhat similar to the 'Who are we?' box in Chapter 2, in that it involves an exchange of images, text etc. The difference now is that we are 'digging deeper' into things that have meaning for the groups in terms of their world and their cultures.

1   Think about the following five categories:
    *   belief
    *   health
    *   fashion
    *   history
    *   performance.

2   In your group, make lists of things that represent each category – text, image, object etc.

3   Choose one item from each list (five in all) and send them to your twin. The items should stand by themselves – do not feel you need to explain

their significance. The function of the items is to arouse the curiosity of your twin.

4   Receive the five items from your twin. Ask questions about the items and send those to your twin – maybe choose those items that particularly interest you and that you would like to know more about, with the possibility that they may be inspirational elements for your play.

5   Create something on the basis of what you have discovered – an improvisation, scene, movement piece, song, dance etc.

6   *Negotiate* with your twin group on five other items and undertake the same process.

Example 24.1

1   Here are examples of items exchanged by two twinned groups around the topics.

Items sent by Chickenshed, UK:

- *Belief*:

    Maybe we have different clothes or skin of a different colour, or we speak different languages. That is on the surface. But basic- ally, we are the same human beings. This is what binds us to each other. That is what makes it possible for us to understand each other and develop friendship and closeness.

    (The Dalai Lama)

- *Health*: the National Health Service logo.
- *Fashion*: a receipt for a pair of trainers.
- *History*: a poppy.
- *Performance*: a photograph of a backstage scene.

Items sent by Tarunya, Bangladesh:

- *Belief*: the word 'liberalism'.
- *Health*: a statement about world pollution.
- *Fashion*: an article about the fusion of eastern and western fashion styles.
- *History*: a photograph of the National Language Monument.
- *Performance*: a photograph of a folk singer.

2   Here is a question about a received item, and how the reply inspired a significant element in the play:

- Chickenshed were interested in the fact that one of their items (the text from the Dalai Lama) included a reference to 'language', and that Tarunya had sent them a photograph of a National Language Monument. Their question was: 'Why do you need to have a monu- ment to your national language?'.

- Tarunya replied by explaining that 'the national language movement is the cornerstone of our national identity'. They explained that Bangladesh is, historically, a relatively new nation (the war of liberation that created it was in 1971), and a key issue in the country is one of national cultural identity. The politics of Bangladesh and the struggles between different factions have been very much bound up with 'language' and 'languages' – which are suppressed, which are 'allowed', which are regarded as the 'voice of the nation'.

- Chickenshed is a mixed-ability company, and the question of 'language' has a special significance for them, in that the use of sign language is a part of their creative process. The play they developed dealt with both the contemporary world and a moment in history (World War II). One scene in the play illustrates how the 'language question' was woven into the play. The scene is set in the 1940s, in London, and is between a young English man and a foreign soldier:

  > Soldier: The fascists took our land from us, Eddie. We must now be a province of *their* country. And then . . . they steal our culture.
  >
  > Eddie: Culture? What's one of them?
  >
  > Soldier: To speak our own language is forbidden. We must speak in their tongue, on fear of death. Can you imagine? No, you are too young. It is a bitter loss. Without language we are not human. So I am here to raise money for weapons. I go back to fight for my language.

Outcome

The exchange of *specific items* and the subsequent questions and replies have produced a rich source of material that can be incorporated into the creative process. We have noted that (as with the case of 'language' in the examples given) there can be a correspondence between the responses exchanged by the twins – thoughts, histories and cultural references achieving a resonance with each other in unexpected and surprising ways.

ROOM FOR DEBATE – CREATIVITY AND DEMOCRATIC HABITS

Democracy. 1. Government by the people or their elected representatives. 2. A political or social unit governed ultimately by all its members. 3. The practice or spirit of social equality.

We hear the word 'democracy' quite a lot these days. America is currently set on exporting it (through the application of force, if need be) to countries and cultures whose histories have not led them down that particular path. In the UK, the government talks of 'protecting our democratic way of life' (while chipping away at the foundation stones of it, some of which were laid down by Magna Carta in 1215). 'Undemocratic' countries, such as Saudi Arabia and Burma, make vague promises of moves towards it, while hanging on to militaristic or monarchist power. But the 'upholders of democracy' merrily make trade- and arms-deals with distinctly undemocratic regimes, and power (political, economic and social) seems to concentrate worldwide into fewer and fewer hands.

Democracy may be many things. An idea or ideal (the 'Liberty, Equality and Fraternity' of the French Revolution). A political system that ensures some degree of equality to all. An ideological or armed struggle for something to be adopted or won (generally won – usually by the spilled blood and determination of the disenfranchised). Whether or not it is the *best* system by which human beings organise themselves is up for dispute (though I personally would prefer to live in a democracy than otherwise). Nelson Mandela clearly believed it was a better option for South Africa than the unfairness of apartheid. Winston Churchill said that, 'It is the worst form of system . . . except for all the others that are on offer'. Some ('undemocratic') societies today look at the freedoms and personal liberties that the western democracies offer and wonder if they are worth aspiring to. The 'freedom' to expose and exploit the human body for commercial gain, to abandon all social restraints, to reject the counsel and wisdom of the elders, to place the individual aspiration above the communal good.

If we look into history, and around the world today, elements of what we call 'democracy' can be found in many unexpected places – and not necessarily just in those countries that declare themselves as 'democracies'. The village council, the collective small agricultural project, the meeting of the elders or the organisation of the household: all places where degrees of equality may be found, no matter what political system they exist under. If it is anything, then, 'democracy' is a *habit*. It is not something that can be exported or imposed: how can the habit of co-operation, collaboration and a spirit of equality be exported or imposed?

The work of artists creating together can be an exercise in the democratic habit. Not always, of course, and I certainly don't want to romanticise 'the arts' as a place where the super-size ego does not exist, or where there are not the most dreadful examples of inequality. There is certainly, in the West (the tradition I work within), a tendency to elevate the 'individual artist' above all else, and to diminish the collective enterprise – even though the absence of the 'individual genius' is evident in many cultures. In your own work, however – this process of creating new theatre through an exchange between different cultures – you are engaged in encouraging this *habit of democracy*. At the core of all the work offered in this book – if it is to achieve its aims – are the principles of:

- listening to, and learning from, 'the other' – as in different views and experiences of the world, possibly radically different from your own;
- adapting your own methods and practices, to absorb and grow from the creative inspirations and insights of 'the different';
- accepting the 'challenge of the new' without retreating into the safety of 'the known';
- learning to articulate and creatively represent one's own experiences to others, with truth and bravery, but without attempting to 'control' those who are receiving them.

Young people are the ones who will be inheriting the future of the world – a world where the need to adapt to new ways of thinking and organising will be crucial, if the world is to survive the perilous turning-point it is at right now. The world needs to listen to them, and to encourage them to engage with each other in ways that are less destructive than the ones we have left them with.

The following activities are offered as ways of exchanging more creative ideas between the groups, through the process of 'The Debating Chamber'

Activity 25 Debating our immediate world

These activities encourage the use of formal (structured) debate to inspire creative material for the narratives being made.

Part one – the formal debate

1   In small groups, make a list of small, achievable things that would make your immediate world (school, district, area) a better place for everyone. This is your 'agenda for change'.

2   Place each agenda item on a separate sheet of paper.

3   As a whole group, feed back the results of the lists (see Example 25.1).

4   Begin to place the separate sheets of paper on the floor. Make groupings of items that have some connection with each other – a 'major agenda' map of generic issues or concerns. See if there are titles for these generic groupings.

5   Identify two or three items from the 'major agenda' that seem to be of most general concern.

6   Take one of the items on the major agenda. You are going to debate ('for' and 'against') the proposal that the item should become a matter of policy.

- Divide the group into two – groups A and B.
- Group A will be proposing the new policy. Discuss the strongest arguments as to why this policy would benefit everyone in the community.

What questions that are of concern to the community does the policy raise and address?

- Group B will be opposing the new policy. Discuss the strongest arguments as to why this policy would have little benefit to the community. What questions has the policy failed to raise and address?

- It does not matter if you *personally* agree or disagree with the subject under debate – the object is to explore as fully as possible all the reasons why the policy should be adopted or not. It is a question of 'placing yourself in the shoes' of someone.

- Elect a speaker from each side to put the case – 'for' or 'against'.

- The speaker can return at times to their support group, for advice on arguments to put forward. Think of the support group as the 'trainers' in a boxing match – giving advice between the 'rounds'. Think of the two speakers as 'the boxers' – going into the ring to use words and ideas to deal the 'knockout argument'.

- During the debate, people may 'cross the floor' to the other side if they find their thoughts and feelings are being swayed.

7   Take a general vote on whether or not the policy should be adopted. This could be done by a formal show of hands, or by creating a circle on the floor: the centre of the circle is an absolute 'yes' vote, the outer ring is an absolute 'no' vote, the points between are the varying degrees of agreement–disagreement.

8   Discuss the thoughts and feelings of those people who have occupied the 'middle ground' of the circle – the 'yes . . . but' votes and the 'no . . . but' votes. These might prove to be the most interesting responses – and perhaps the territory where some form of consensus might be arrived at.

Part two – the informal debate

The 'formal debate' will now provide you with material for a dramatic scene. Take the item that has been debated and explore how the different sides of the argument might take place in a less formal setting.

1   You are going to create a dramatic scene that focusses on the issue in hand. You will be able to use all of the skills and activities that you have developed through the activities in the book so far.

2   Create a family grouping. Decide on:

- who is being represented – try for as wide a range of characters and ages as possible; thinking about previous activities, be specific about the types of people they are, what their economic circumstances are etc.;

- where they are and what they are doing as a group – are they in the home, in a public place, at a particular event?; again, remind your-selves of previous activities such as the dramatic use of location, event etc.
- how the issue will be raised in the scene: who will be 'for' the new idea and who will be 'against' it?; who will change their mind?

Draw all of the arguments that have been already rehearsed in the 'formal debate' in the previous activity – this is your major resource for the scene.

3   *Exchange* with your twin:
- the original lists of 'major agenda' items;
- the issue that was chosen for debate;
- the scene you have created around the issue.

4   Look at the scene your twin has created. It will probably be about a different issue, and it will be a different family. You are going to develop your original scene by incorporating a character from the scene your twin has created. Do this by:

- deciding which character from the scene your twin has created you will introduce into your own scene; how did they come to be there – a visiting friend, relation or guest, a stranger who becomes involved in the situation, someone who has turned up unex-pectedly?;
- discovering how the incorporation of the new person affects the movement of the scene;
- what new thoughts, feelings and perspectives are added to this 'family debate'?;
- if there are language differences, seeing how this affects the scene; do the different meanings behind words in translation affect the outcome of the debate?

5   *Exchange* the adapted scenes with your twin.

Example 25.1

Here are some of the agenda items of local concern that were put forward by the youth theatre at The Performing Arts Centre, Amman, Jordan, during one twinning project. The formal debates that could take place around these topics would provide splendid material for 'informal debate' dramatic scenes.

- Paint the houses in the poorer areas.
- Create a green belt around Amman.
- Make more places for teenagers to spend their time.

- Reduce the number of plastic bags that swamp the streets.
- Reduce the smog that settles on the city.
- Stop shooting guns in the air at wedding ceremonies (a cultural custom).

Outcome

In the formal debate, the group will have experienced:

- identifying things that could make a better immediate social environment for everyone;
- arguing a strong case for and against something, within a framework that allows everyone to express their thoughts and feelings, questions and attitudes;
- accepting that there might not be an absolute 'yes' or 'no' answer or vote.

The informal debate has:

- created a living, dramatic scene from the material provided by the formal debate; it has shown that theatre has the ability to explore big 'public' issues through the detail of people's personal and private lives;
- shown how – by adapting a scene to incorporate someone from another community or culture – our views of the world can gain another perspective.

Activity 26 Debating our wider world

Apply the same techniques to agenda items that apply to the lives of everyone beyond the immediate locality or community – concerns of national importance. Try for things that seem achievable and specific – 'Teach more foreign languages in schools' has a specific aim and could become a policy, whereas 'Be more interested in foreigners' is not something that could be legislated for.

Activity 27 Debating our shared world

Adapt the same techniques to incorporate the suggestions of both groups from the start.

1   *Exchange* lists of agenda items between the twins. Make one long list of all the items suggested. Again, try for things that are specific, but don't limit your ambitions: think big (see Example 27.1).

2   Each group should create its own maps of 'major agenda' items and select the ones that seem of most general concern.

3   *Exchange* the selected major agendas and agree on *one* of them for both groups to work with in the formal debate.

4   *Exchange* the results of the formal debates.

5   Each group is to create its own informal debate scenes.

6   *Exchange* the informal debate scenes.

7   Adapt the formal debate scenes by introducing a character or characters from the scene created by the twin group.

Example 27.1

Here is a list of combined agenda items from different groups, all of them addressing things that could be implemented across the world. Some of them might seem fanciful, mischievous or non-achievable – but . . .

*   Create a United Nations of Young People organisation.
*   Publish the names of all companies that manufacture land-mines.
*   Stop buying 'celebrity magazines' for a week.
*   Make drama and music the core subjects in every school.
*   Create a 'human chain' of linked hands across the world.
*   Create a small international vocabulary, so that everyone in the world has the same words for phrases such as 'Let us be friends'.
*   Create an 'Emperor's new clothes' bomb. It doesn't kill or harm people in the slightest way – just makes them look foolish (as in a cartoon, where the person ends up with clothes in shreds and their hair standing on end). Aim it at people in power who like to look dignified in their robes of state and uniforms covered in medals, but who do things that harm lives.
*   Stop killing elephants.

Cross-reference

See Activities 36 and 59.

COMMENT – ASPECTS OF WORK IN THE CHAPTER

It has changed the lives of our participants which, in turn . . . changes the lives of our communities.

(Live Theatre, UK)

For us, as an organization, it has opened up a discussion about the importance of looking at youth culture and the specific problems of young people and young artists, which, in this part of the world, is virtually absent.

(Kattaikkuttu Sangam, India)

I'm much more confident to explore themes and issues that exist currently around the world.

(Chickenshed Youth Theatre, UK)

An exchange of video or film about the companies can help. Simple things such as how we wear our hair or the clothes we wear can make the exchange seem much more personal. It is helpful to hear the twins speaking too – the tones they use when talking say much, even if they are speaking in a language you don't know.

(Company member, Contact, UK)

When we were sending our twin a particular theatre game – they were in India and we were in the UK – we asked ourselves if it might contain things that offended them. We didn't want them to feel we were insulting their culture. As it was, they were fine about it. What was weird is that we discovered that we were sending things to our twin in Asia that did not upset them, but that those same things might upset Asians here in the UK.

(Company member, Contact, UK)

4 Getting the story

At a certain stage of your process you will arrive at the point where you begin to *commit to the story*. When and how this happens will depend on the scope and time-scale of your twinning and on the nature of your group. The nine-month long project will have more time to land on a particular narrative than the one-month long project. A group that meets on a formal, once-weekly basis may have more time constraints on it than the group that has a more daily or informal working process. The length of time needed for a full rehearsal period needs to be taken into account.

Before we look at activities that begin to shape the final story, here are some general points of guidance:

- Although the *process* of the twinning (the creative exchange and mutual inspiration) is the heart of the project, the groups need to maintain a focus on where it is leading. The thrill and joy of 'putting on a show' are things that link the child acting out a story in the playground directly with the grand actor strutting the stage of a national theatre. In our process we should never lose sight of this, and we should beware of the process work becoming a seemingly endless succession of tasks with no end in sight. Therefore the advice is always to *do something* with the creative material received from the twin group – to find ways in which to inspire a drama activity.
- Following on from the above, the timing of when we commit to the final story is key: how long to 'hold off' and when to 'foreclose'. To hold off too long can result in the drive and impetus of the project being lost; to foreclose too soon can lose some of the creative riches that the exchange offers. In my experience of a range of twinning projects, the timing for the emergence of the final story – or its general outlines – should happen somewhere between the *one-third* and *halfway* points in the process. Even then, there can still be a fluidity and an openness to development,

but the outlines of 'the show' – the characters, the story, the *drama* – will be there, beckoning us on to that thrilling moment when all is revealed to an expectant audience.

- The groups will need to negotiate the timing of this *commitment to story* very carefully. In terms of the schedule of the project this is perhaps the key moment. A group that has worked together for a long time may have the experience and confidence to arrive at a story outline very quickly. However, they may be twinned with a group that has just formed, who are still finding their way and need a longer gestation period. What should be avoided are feelings of either 'they are holding us back' or 'they are pushing us too fast'.

- A determining factor in the above will also be the *structure(s)* of the final plays. The twins who elect to write a single play together will have a different task to those whose plays are different in outline, even if they share similar themes. Chapter 8 will look at structure in more detail and how that impacts upon the collaborative process.

- No matter how all of the above is dealt with, the stress should always be on the continuing process of *incorporating* the work of the twin into the final piece of work. The bravest work I have seen has taken this 'up to the wire'. Two groups had been working with each other, at long-range, over a period of months. They had agreed on a structure that incorporated scenes from each other's plays and knew they had to have a final scene that brought both plays together. The end of the project was for the two groups finally to meet, dress-rehearse their two plays and perform them the following day. On the evening before the performance, they created their final (joint) scene together. This was a decidedly high-risk strategy, but it worked – and it did so because of the mutual trust that had been built up between the two groups during the process. Not all projects will follow this course, but the aspiration should always be to 'stay open' for as long as possible.

The activities in this chapter will look at the range of different elements that go into finding the story:

- the thing that inspires you;
- character(s);
- subject matter;
- narrative;
- setting or location(s);
- theme(s).

Before you look at the activities below, here is a major note of advice. The six elements identified above are dealt with in the order of the list I have made. But in terms of the 'spark of inspiration' that fuels a story, they should not be seen as a 'set in stone' schematic approach. For instance, you might find that your initial inspiration comes from the image of a *location*, even if you have no idea of who the characters might be or what the subject matter of the story will be. You might have an enthusiasm for a particular *theme*, even if you have no idea where the story will be set. My advice is to *go with the inspiration*. So – in engaging with the activities below – always bear in mind that you can dip in and out of them as you see fit.

Some of the activities in this chapter will follow on from those in previous chapters, others will be new ones.

Section one – the thing that inspires you

Before we look at the elements that go into making a new story, there is something very important to remember – it is the one you *need* to tell. Any writer will confirm this. There is no point in embarking on the journey if you feel that it is something you *should* do, or *ought* to do. This must apply equally to a group enterprise. You may follow the guidance given in this book all you like, but if you do not have a genuine enthusiasm for the story (and only you will know if that is present), all you will have is a set of exercises turned into play form. This is why some plays can be well constructed, have important things to say and cannot be faulted in many ways, yet seem to have no 'heart'.

So, throughout your process – particularly during the early activities, where you are creating and exchanging material – be constantly on the lookout for the thing that leaps out at you and says '*this* is the seed of the story we want to make'. It might be a 'big subject' (the effects of globalisation on people's lives, as seen through the eyes of people working in call centres), or a very small image or object (a deserted stadium, a pebble from a beach). It might be a 'hidden history' (a detail of local or national history that is shouting out to be acknowledged), or a new thought that has been expressed by someone from another culture ('How do men and women interact within a religious space?'). Whatever it is – or they are – hang onto them. Don't attempt to 'justify' them – often the most seemingly trivial or unimportant idea for a story can prove to be the seed of a great new narrative. Jot all the ideas down and see if the seeds grow.

Activity 28 Seeds of stories

1   Keep a list or a log book of possible seeds for a story. At the end of each session, discuss what things have caught your attention – either from material you have created or from material sent by your twin – and could be the starting point for a story. Don't worry if it is not clear *how* the story will happen; the important thing is that there is something in the idea that excites you at the moment.

2   *Exchange* the ideas with your twin. Do you have similar thoughts? Which of your thoughts interest your twin? Which of your twin's thoughts interest you?

Section two – character

Many of the previous activities have suggested a diversity of characters, all inspired by creative material exchanged by the twins. Some have been 'thumbnail sketches', and others have been the fuller outlines. Here we will be creating a character or characters that both groups share.

Activity 29 A shared character

Together with your twin you are going to create a character. This character will:

*   appear in both your plays – possibly as *exactly the same person* or as a *similar type of person*;
*   have a significant role in the story of the play – either as a *central character* or as someone who is somehow *important to the story*;
*   be developed through memories and stories from your own lives, which are shared with your twin;
*   be either the starting-point for the story that is to be told, or – if the story has already begun to be developed – be 'dropped into' the narrative.

1   With your twin, negotiate one *type of person* you are going to create to-gether. Choose someone who could be *significant* or *important* to the life of a young person. Agree on a gender for this person (see Example 29.1).

2   In your group, each participant should think about the type of person you have chosen with your twin. For example, if you have chosen to create a grandfather with your twin, think of your own grandfather, or a grandfather that you know.

3   Use your own memories and experience to answer the following questions about the character. Each participant should answer every question. You just need to give brief answers – a word or a sentence. These are the *facts about the character*. Someone in the group should keep a record of everyone's answers.

    *   What physical characteristic or body part do you most identify with this person?
    *   What object do you most identify with this person?
    *   What smell do you most identify with this person?
    *   What word or phrase do you most identify with this person (in their own language)?
    *   What is this person's special place?
    *   What is this person's hobby?
    *   What does this person love?
    *   What does this person fear?
    *   What does this person dream of at night?

- What is this person's most important memory?
- What is this person's ambition?
- What place in the world would this person love to be in?

See Example 29.2.

4 Make full lists of all the answers. Exchange them with your twin. Add the lists of your twin to your own. Include everything and resist the temptation to edit anything that seems contradictory. They will be long lists – and they are now *all the facts about the character*. Some of the 'facts' will not seem to 'fit' together – particularly if they have come from two very different cultures. This might at first seem problematic, but it is what will make the character totally unique.

5 Each twin will now have the same lists. In your group, using all the information you have, explore the character in whatever way you wish. For example:

- Write the character's diary.
- Make a 'who am I?' box (as in Activity 2) for the character.
- Try out the character's hobbies.
- Act out the character's dreams.
- Write a speech for the character using their words and phrases.
- 'Hot seat' the character. A member of the group sits in a chair, as the character. In character, he or she answers questions put by the rest of the group. The person who is in the 'hot seat' should not resist the questions – don't block or evade (think of the people who are questioning you – that is 'the character' – as friends and not judges).

6 In continuing to develop the character there will certainly be a *selecting of material*. The twin groups might decide to share *exactly the same material*, to share only *some of the material* or to make their *own selections*. Whatever is decided upon, it is important to include equal amounts of your twin group's 'facts' and your own.

7 Looking at all the 'facts about the character' and the results of the explorations, start to develop a life history that weaves together all the things that seem not to 'fit in' or to be contradictory. Don't try to 'iron out' what seems to be problematic – use it as a creative inspiration. Add new things in order to link the material together, but make sure that the key aspects of the character are drawn from the work that has been developed through the exchange. Attempt several thumbnail sketches of the character to see which might provide the greatest dramatic opportunities (see Example 29.3).

8 Develop other characters, using similar techniques. These may be characters or character types that you are not personally familiar with, in which case some research will be necessary. Always embrace the things that seem contradictory and use them creatively. Always head for the thumbnail sketches to see what the dramatic potential is (see Example 29.4).

9   It may be that the twins decide upon a character or character type that can be found in both cultures, but where there are specific *cultural differences* that you would like to retain. For instance a *busker* (*street artist*) in Brazil would have a different 'profile' to one in the UK. In this case, there may be some sharing of characteristics, but without losing the *cultural specificity* of the characters (see Example 29.5).

10   See if any of the characters inspire other aspects of the play – subject matter, topic, issue, themes etc. (see Example 29.6).

Example 29.1

- a grandfather
- a male teacher
- an older sister
- a female novelist
- a male explorer.

Example 29.2

Here are some examples of complete lists of facts about a *grandfather*. Note how different cultural elements or references go to make up the whole person.

1   Some of the objects most identified with the grandfather:
- a pipe
- a banjo
- a walking stick
- a djembe (African drum)
- bagpipes (Scottish musical wind instrument)
- brown woollen jumper
- a 'Best Bet' horse-racing booklet.

2   Some words or phrases associated with the grandfather:
- '*Oa mai oe*' ('How are you' in Samoan)
- 'Aye, why aye, why bloody aye, bloody students!'
- 'When I was your age . . .'
- '*To e pe fo'i pea tau tuku*' ('One more row to dig and then we're done boys' in Tongan).

3   Some of the grandfather's most important memories:
- getting a medal from the Queen of England
- fishing with his son
- meeting his wife in wartime France
- walking up Wellington Hill in New Zealand.

4   Some of the grandfather's ambitions:
   • to make it to the toilet
   • to write a book
   • to walk the Himalayas
   • to live to be 100 years old.

Example 29.3

Here are some examples of thumbnail sketches about the grandfather's life. They are different ways of drawing together, into a single character, different cultural references in a way that is both believable and unique. Any of them could be the starting-point for a story or for a character that is central or significant to a story in some way.

• A very old man is walking up Wellington Hill in New Zealand. He is talking to his son about his life. He is Scottish and fought in France in the First World War. He was part of the infantry band and played his bagpipes at dawn. While in France – on leave in a village behind the battle-lines – he met his future wife. In later years they settled in New Zealand. At the top of the hill he says that, before he reaches the age of 100, he wants to walk the Himalayas. At this very moment, though, he does not look too happy. 'Oa mai oe?' his son asks. He says he wants to get back down the hill and find a toilet.

• A young New Zealand man goes to Europe to fight in the First World War. He takes his banjo with him. He is later presented with a medal from the Queen for his bravery. He was famous in the ranks as the soldier who – when the troops were ordered to go into battle – would cry out 'To e pe fo'i pea tau tuku'. He decides to stay in England and joins a circus, where he meets an African drummer and a Scottish bagpipe player. They form a band, but have no success. When they part company, his friends give him their instruments.

• An old man owns an antique shop. The only three things he refuses to sell are an African drum, a set of bagpipes and a banjo. Every lunchtime he goes out to place a bet on the horse races, taking his tips from a 'Best Bet' booklet.

Example 29.4

Here are some examples of short character sketches developed by groups who have been involved in twinning projects. They each contain 'facts' drawn from lists made by both twins.

• The taxi-driver smells of braai (South African barbeque). He says 'Masambe' and 'I'll tell you what the problem is!' He dreams of missed opportunities and is afraid of pigeons because they remind him of the old (apartheid) police uniform.

- The professor smells of honesty and chocolate. His special place is an armchair in a courtyard in an isolated village. He dreams of someone running away from his outstretched arms.

- The busker often says, 'What does not make sense you will understand. What you don't understand will make sense'. His special place is the top of a building, with a deckchair and an ashtray.

- The grandmother lies in bed in her flat in Glasgow. She wants to go out and walk in Rouken Glen park, but is too ill. All she can do is watch the television. A programme about Rwanda comes on. She remembers her youth, when she met another young woman, who was from that land, and shared a drink of whisky with her. She wonders how and where she is.

Example 29.5

Two groups – Novos Novos (Brazil) and Young Blood (UK) – decided to create the character of a *busker* (street artist). The character was to become central to the final plays. One of them would be living in the UK and one would be living in Salvador. The creative exchange activity was to discover what the two characters had in common, and what the cultural differences were. The research techniques included:

- spending time investigating the lives of real-life buskers or street artists in Leicester and Salvador; their personal and public lives; family and friends; stories they have; the people around them on the street;

- inviting a busker into a group session to talk to the group, lead a workshop;

- learning a song, routine or act from a busker;

- recording a 'day in the life' of a busker – video, audio, writing, drawing;

- exchanging with the twin group the similarities and differences between the buskers in Leicester and Salvador. It was discovered that the '*Repentista*' or '*Cigana*' from Salvador is very different from the guitar player or mime artist on the streets of Leicester in terms of cultural specificity. But the experience of being on the streets, earning a living (or not) from the kindness of strangers, was not so different. Difficulties expressed by buskers in the UK were reflected in a remark by a Brazilian busker:

> I work very much every days. So I hate when one people ignore my work. Just would give any opinions of what I did. But nothing. They look at me, look to other place for don't see me, and go in front.

Example 29.6

Here is an example of a character that opened the door for the development of the full, final plays.

Two groups – Art of the Street, Grahamstown, South Africa and Act2LDN, London, UK – decided to create *a taxi-driver* as a central character for their plays. As in Example 29.5, there was a mixture of similarities and cultural specificity.

The South African taxi-driver:

- Interviews revealed the problems of violence facing taxi-drivers in Grahamstown, and the very real threat of being killed in rivalries between taxi associations. However, one taxi-driver said his most important memory was, 'when rival taxi associations achieved unity and began to combat the violence'.

- The subject matter of taxi-transport as mediators for people attending important events began to emerge from the research. This gave rise to the idea of an 'organising principle' for the play – the passage involved in the rites of marriage, death and birth.

- The image of a 'magical taxi' arose: the taxi that could fly. Where would it go, and who would decide?

The UK taxi-driver:

- Research involved work around 'the Knowledge' – the test that the London cab driver has to take in order to obtain a licence. The Knowledge requires the driver be familiar with the London routes in great detail.

- This gave rise to an interest in the geography of London and, in particular, the river that divides the city both literally and metaphorically. Maps, journeys and destinations emerged as subject matters for the play: 'you may know somewhere like the back of your hand, but even if you know all the routes you can still lose your way'.

Outcome

- The twinned groups will now share a character – or character type – that appears in both their plays.

- The character may be the starting point for the story, or will be 'dropped into' the story.

- Other characters may be shared in a similar way.

- The character has been created not just through the work in this chapter, but also through any of the activities in previous chapters that are useful. The *process of creative exchange* is therefore fully embedded in the *final outcome*.

Activity 30 The characters speak

A play can be seen as a type of experiment: observing *human beings in action*. That is, human beings 'doing' – physically, emotionally or psychologically. This applies to all live drama, whatever form it takes – social realism, abstract narratives, verbal or non-verbal theatre. It is always people *being active*.

1   Think about the character you are developing. Think about previous activities you have undertaken that involve the particular uses of language (the use of questions, for example, or what happens with language when people are 'debating').

2   What words or turns of phrase do you hear the character using most frequently? Words that might suggest what thought processes, emotions, ways of expressing themselves etc. are typical of them? What words and phrases give a clue as to what might be their psychological 'actives'.

3   Use a mixture of words and phrases from your own language culture and from that of your twin.

Cross-reference

See Activity 49.

Activity 31 One character, different voices

In terms of plays that use words, if we are looking at how we 'get the story', it is worthwhile thinking a little of not just *what* the characters are saying, but *how* they are saying it.

We often think of a person as always speaking in a certain way, and in the previous activity we looked at how a character may have 'characteristic words' or turns of phrase that mark them out individually. But if we consider it (and if we think about ourselves), people also have different *modes* of speaking, depending on the *context* they are in. The mother making breakfast for her children will speak in a different way to the manner (words, rhythms, syntax) she will employ when she is speaking at a board meeting at work. A man talking to his servant will speak in a different way from when he is trying to seduce his friend. If I am speaking at a public meeting, I will not be speaking as I would to my mother (unless, of course, my mother says 'You always talk to me as if you are speaking to a public meeting'!) If you are trying to communicate with someone whose language you are unfamiliar with, you probably won't speak in the way that you do to the policeman who is arresting you. One hopes that the Queen of England doesn't speak to her children in the same way as she speaks when she is opening Parliament.

All these (and all other) *modes of language* tell an aspect of the story of a person. And this applies, of course, to characters in plays. In the course of one day (or in one play), a person or a character may express themselves in a range of modes – formal, informal, colloquial, confident, intimate, public, technical, casual etc.

If, in our creative exchange of work with our twin group, we are building characters together (as in the previous exercise) and we are exploring the journeys of those characters, we might begin to think about how those journeys may be expressed through the different modes they speak in.

1   Take a character from your play and see how they use language differently in different situations, or at different times in their lives. Improvise or write short scenes. You might try this with one actor representing all the different aspects of the character, or different actors for each different aspect. Try some of the following:

   •   The character is in a position of authority or high status – perhaps as an elder in the community, or a leader in their group.
   •   The character is in a situation where they have low status and little authority – perhaps they are in the hands of the police, or being punished by the head teacher.
   •   The character is very confident – perhaps they are in their own community, where they know all the codes of behaviour and language (when shopping, or travelling etc.).
   •   The character is very unconfident – perhaps they are in a foreign setting, where they do not know the codes of behaviour and have very little of the language.
   •   The character is 'the teacher' – perhaps introducing a visitor from another culture to their community.
   •   The character is 'the taught' – perhaps being introduced to another culture or community.
   •   The character is in a situation where they have very fixed and rigid opinions – where they 'know' they are right.
   •   The character is in a situation where their fixed opinions are challenged – where their view of something begins to change.
   •   The character is behaving in a very cruel or unkind way.
   •   The character is behaving in a very sympathetic or kind way.
   •   The character communicates in a non-verbal language: signed speaking, or through improvised gesture.

2   Try any of the above with different characters in your story.

3   *Exchange* with your twin group some of the different 'language situations' for *one* of your characters.

4   Create situations between your character and the one from your twin. Create a scene or scenes between them. *Exchange* these with your twin.

Outcome

The activity has:

- shown that 'one person is many people', depending on the situation they are in;

- questioned the notion of the 'fixed personality' – how human nature is fluid, and our behaviour and language can shift dramatically from one situation to another;

- illuminated a key element in making a dramatic narrative – *how and why people change*;

- begun to draw together characters from the different stories being developed by the twins.

Cross-reference

See Activity 49.

Section three – subject matter

The subject matter of a play is what the story (narrative) is based on – the 'topic', the 'issue' or the 'areas of concern' are all different terms we can use for this. We have seen in the previous activity how research into a character or character type can suggest the subject matter for a narrative. Here are some suggestions as to how to find your subject matter even before you have found your characters.

Activity 32 Reviewing the activities

1   Work in small groups. Each group takes one exchange activity from the work that has been done so far.

2   Use your own material (sent to your twin) and your twin's material (received by you).

3   Make lists of 'topics', 'issues' or 'areas of concern' that are suggested by the creative material inspired by the activities.

4   As a whole group, make one long list of the topics etc. that have come up. Make groups of topics that seem to 'attach' to each other.

5   *Exchange* your lists – and 'attached groupings' – with your twin.

6   *Negotiate* with your twin on certain subject matters that interest you both.

7   See if there is *one specific subject matter area* that you wish to explore more deeply, as a basis for a narrative. It might be that each twin chooses a different subject matter, particular to its own culture. But the sharing of it will create a fresh basis for further interaction between the groups.

Example 32.1

Here are some examples of *specific subject matter areas* arising from the activity.

- separation, walls, the partition of countries (inspired by an image of bricks): *a company from India*;

- the rights and freedoms of women in society (inspired by the object of a diaphragm – a female contraceptive device): *a company from India*;

- the transition from the rural to the urban due to economic pressures (inspired by images of the countryside and of cities): *a company from Nigeria*;

- economic dependency on richer nations (inspired by the image of suitcases and the phrase 'many suitcases brought in, filled with things bought cheap in the American market and resold here'): *a company from Trinidad and Tobago*;

- pollution of the environment and public health (inspired by the accounts of health hazards on the underground transport system): *a company from the UK*.

Activity 33 Narrowing the frame

Let us assume that you have identified subject matters – topics, issues, areas of concern – that you are interested in exploring further. The task now is to 'narrow the frame' of the research – to find a *specific* subject matter that interests the group and see how this can become a frame for the story.

1 Decide on the general subject matter that the play will be dealing with.

2 Identify a particular *situation, instance or circumstance* within which to explore the subject matter creatively. You may choose something that is very local to you, or something that is rooted in history or another culture.

3 Set the group research tasks that are appropriate and useful to the exploration. If you have chosen a situation, event or circumstance that is rooted in history, or in another culture, this will perhaps require a greater depth of research. But even if you have chosen something that is more local and contemporary (and therefore more familiar), don't assume that you have all the knowledge and information you need. Remember Activity 23 – the 'hidden histories' – and how our immediate, daily world contains a wealth of new knowledge (see Examples 33.1 and 33.2).

4 Devise your own creative activities to add dramatic flesh to the research you have done (see Example 33.3).

5 Write an opening scene based on everything you have done (see Example 33.4).

Example 33.1

The following work was undertaken by a group involved in a twinning project:

Chickenshed, London, UK

This is an example of some of the research work undertaken by a group that had chosen *Pollution of the environment and public health* as their subject matter. Their *specific circumstance* was the underground transport system. Their research included the following:

- The findings concerning conditions on the underground system from the 'hidden histories', in Activity 23.

- An official report on air quality and Tube rage. The report advised that tube rage would rise unless air quality was improved. It called for immediate improvement in the ventilation systems.

- A statement from the Director of the British Association of Anger Management said: 'A reduction in the level of oxygen in an enclosed space leads to increasing feelings of panic . . . an individual can experience reactions such as anxiety, aggression, impatience and feelings of sickness'.

- A spokesperson for London Underground said, 'The company is examining ways of improving ventilation'.

- Another report stated that, 'It is very unlikely that tunnel dust on the underground has any serious adverse affect on the health of Tube passengers and staff'.

- Newspaper reports and headlines on incidents on the underground.

- Records kept by the group of specific journeys made. The actual experience of being on the underground system. 'The dull acrid smell . . . which is also the smell of London dust and burnt London hair . . . the clinging odor of the morning rush hour, leaving a metallic quality at the back of the throat'.

Example 33.2

This is an example of what 'historical research' can unearth.

- The Chickenshed group became interested in the histories of the London Underground. The research into this – while not distracting from the subject matter of pollution and public health – took the work into new (though related) areas.

- During World War II, the London Underground system was used as public bomb shelters. They were often overcrowded and unhealthy. Many of these shelters were hit by bombs, and many people died. In terms of the subjects of 'pollution' and 'health', there is a direct

resonance here with a contemporary look at conditions on the underground system. The American soldier who, viewing the situation of the
people in these shelters, said 'I don't know how you put up with this'
could well be voicing the modern-day person entering the dirty and
dangerous conditions of some of the stations.

Example 33.3

Here is some of the creative task devised by Chickenshed to create dramatic
moments from the research work done on contemporary conditions in the
London Underground:

- An improvisation – everyone squashed on a packed Tube train. Someone
  is trying to travel in peace and quiet, reading their book. What is the
  book? Does it contain a narrative that is at odds with the environment
  (peaceful and tranquil) or reflects it (dangerous and aggressive)?
- In small groups, create a non-verbal sequence using newspapers, bags
  and book etc. Use words such as impatience, patience, not caring, personal space, tolerance, manners etc. as a starting-point.
- Create a movement piece using the following physical gestures as a
  starting point: scoop, twist, squash, twitch, shove etc.
- Take one of the sequences and add verbal elements: quotes from newspaper articles on Tube rage, quotes from a book that is being read,
  random thoughts, announcements over the public-address system etc.
- Develop all of the above into an abstract sequence – the 'essence' of
  being in the situation. Allow it to develop a rhythm, perhaps on a 'loop'.

Other possibilities would be:

- 'Freeze frame' the action and allow characters to talk about themselves.
- Add in one of the developed characters from the earlier activity in this
  chapter (what would the South African taxi-driver make of this situation
  if he found himself in it, for instance?).

Example 33.4

Here is an opening scene written by Chickenshed, UK. Some things to note
are:

- It is based upon the subject matter the group decided upon (pollution,
  health).
- It develops from the creative exercises they based upon their research.

- It incorporates material from the 'belief, health, fashion, history and performance' exercise in Activity 24. In particular, the subject matter of the Chickenshed play was prompted by their twin's item on world pollution that came out of the exercise.

- It provides the key setting/location for the play – a good example in itself of how the discovery of the key elements for the story do not necessarily make themselves known in a schematic manner.

- The title of the play – 'On the surface' – was inspired by a quote from the Dalai Lama. The quote and the title became one of the central themes of the play – again, a good example of how 'theme' can be arrived at through unexpected inspiration, and not in a schematic way.

The scene has been slightly edited down here, and some stage directions have been simplified.

'ON THE SURFACE'

Scene 1: A carriage in an underground train.

Three people open newspapers:

One: a middle-class woman in conservative-type clothes; the *Daily Telegraph*;
Two: a plainly dressed female office worker; the *Daily Mail*;
Three: a young working man with his bag of tools; the *Sun*.

They read out their headlines. They are ignored by the other passengers, who avoid eye contact or read books etc.

Between each sequence of headlines, there are group-choreographed stumblings and lurchings as the train moves.

DT: Time for the government to say it's sorry.
DM: Ninety-year-old jogger crushed by a lorry.
SUN: Porn star lands a new role in 'Corrie' [a soap opera].

DM and SUN turn pages.

DM: Immigrant dentist is king of the scroungers.
SUN: Footballer crippled in sex romp on lounger.

All turn pages.

DT: Security forces seek Afghanistani.
DM: Fashion season kicks off with Armani.
SUN: Mother of three finds snake in her sarnie!

Others respond to the Sun.

DT: Unions back down as crisis nears.
DM: Killer driver has twenty one beers.
SUN: 'Big Brother' sex orgy ends up in tears.

All turn page. Increased interest in the Sun *from others.*

DT: Later retirement for baby boomers.
DM: Spicy food can cause cancerous tumours.
SUN: TV presenter denied lesbian rumours.

Expressions of interest from others.

DT: Armament stockpile could be Al Quaeda's.
DM: Two years inside for 'inhuman' dog breeders.
SUN: Eastender [soap opera] star strips off for our readers!

All turn page. Cheers from others.

DT: Global warming result of increased pollution.
DM: Energy minister accused of collusion.
SUN: Okay, we'll all fry, but what's the solution?

All in the train begin to fan themselves. The readers get more urgent.

DT: London Tube to face next attack?

All others take full notice, some showing concern.

DM: Rail tragedy blamed for worn out track.

All show increased alarm.

SUN: Suicide bombs found in old rucksack.

Passengers cower and look afraid.

DT: (Shouts) Rail pile up due to criminal error.

Passengers moan.

DM: Maniac axe-man in underground terror!

All scream. Increased panic. The train slows, all lurch forward. An announcement on the tannoy.

ANN: The next station is Kings Cross.

All climb over each other to get out. The Sun *reader is oblivious.*

SUN: Today's astrology. 'You will be undertaking a long and interesting journey'.
ANN: Mind the gap.

Section four – narrative

At this point in the process, the twinned groups will be starting to fully develop their narratives. One danger is that the exchange process can take a back seat if we are not careful. So this a useful moment to remind ourselves of certain 'ground rules' or agreed first principles that have gone into the project – and that should be maintained throughout the process:

- Material received from the twin is fully incorporated into the play we are making. The nature of this material will depend on the activities you have chosen to share with each other, but whatever it is should be there as *essential to the story* and not as an 'add on'.
- Characters may have been created together – whether 'composite characters' or culturally specific characters that have some things in common. Again, these characters need to be *essential to the story*, even if they are not the central character in the play.
- The subject matter of the two plays may be different, but they should – in some way – reflect or resonate with each other.
- The narratives of the plays may be different in outline, but they should also – in some way – reflect or resonate with each other.
- The process of exchange should continue, even though there may be a divergence of 'story' between the two plays.
- In terms of the previous point, the *structural models* of the plays will have a big influence on the continuing exchange. This aspect of the work is looked at in detail in Chapter 8.

The twins who decide to create one single play together will have a different task to the twins who are developing different plays but with a shared theme. But in all cases, it is important to keep in mind that the *process should be fully embodied in the final work*. This is what makes a creative twinning project unique among all the different ways of creating new theatre – it is indeed pioneering work and pushes at the boundaries of how theatre that is reflective of our shared world is made.

The narrative of a play is the 'what happens' aspect of it – the unfolding sequence of dramatic events. We have already considered one way of thinking about a play: *human behaviour in action*. In the previous activities, both in this chapter and the earlier ones, there have been many examples of how 'dramatic event' can evolve. We have also seen how a *specific situation*, based on a *general subject matter*, can begin to develop the narrative outlines for a whole play.

Activity 34 A full story

You may now have developed a character or characters, discovered a subject matter and begun to explore dramatic moments. You may have already done some work around other sections that come later in this chapter – setting (location) and theme. Now see if – on the basis of any or all of these – you can begin to develop the outline for a full story.

1   Develop a number of possible story outlines, keeping them as brief as possible. Don't worry if there are gaps – just go for something that:
    •   is firmly rooted in all the work you have done so far;
    •   has an observable narrative drive to it.
    See Example 34.1.

2   Choose one of the outlines that particularly interests you – something that makes you think, 'Yes, there's a good story inside this'. Send it to your twin.

3   Receive your twin's outline.

4   See if the two different outlines resonate with each other. See if aspects of the two outlines could interact with each other – or be woven together in some way. As with the 'creating a joint character' activity earlier in this chapter, do not be put off by things that don't seem to 'fit together' or feel contradictory. As we have seen, it is often these things that can be the most creatively inspiring.

5   Continue to develop your narrative as a group, devising new ways of seeking inspiration from your twin.
    See Example 34.2.

Example 34.1

Here are three story-line options developed by a group involved in a twinning project – a primary class in Nottingham, UK. The options were developed out of the creative exchange with another primary class in Norfolk, UK.

1   Two tribes meet. Some of the people like each other, some of the people dislike each other. Some people are called traitors.

2   There is only one book left in the whole world. It contains the history of the whole world. Two tribes go into battle to decide which tribe the book belongs to.

3   A group of people don't want to take sides, even though they belong to different tribes. They make a journey to another part of the world, where they can live in peace.

Example 34.2

Here is an example of two groups who decided to create one play together: Mashrika, Kigali, Rwanda, and MacRobert, Stirling, UK. Note how a shared character was key to the development of the narrative.

Both groups decided to use a 'grandmother' figure in their plays.

- Mashrika sent stories of their own grandmothers to their twin. One story was about a grandmother who would not allow her grandchildren to eat her precious groundnuts.

- MacRobert acted out some of the stories, adapting some of the details to their own culture – African groundnuts were changed to Scottish oats.

- Both groups named their grandmother figures. Each group gave their grandmother a middle name suggested by their twin.

- The groups took the dilemmas of each other's grandmothers and transferred them to their own contemporary cultures and contexts.

- The groups decided to link the story of a Scottish grandmother with the story of a Rwandan grandmother (and her granddaughter):

  > The death of her husband leaves Grandmother Ignatius Smith with the opportunity to visit her old friend in Rwanda. But much has changed since they shared that bottle of Scotch in a rural Irish station so many years ago. When family pressures stop Nana in her tracks, she devises a way to accomplish her task – her journey – setting in motion a train of events that change more than one life.

  > An orphaned child in Rwanda lives on the streets. One day, through chance circumstance, she meets an old woman from Scotland – a place she has never been to, but has heard of from her grandmother (now dead). Gradually, the older and the younger piece together a history they share through the dead woman. Memories are revived for the Scottish woman, and a turning point in life arrives for the child.

Cross-reference

See Chapter 8 and Activity 59.

Section five – setting or location

Where the play is set – the location(s) in which the drama unfolds – is as vital as anything else in the telling of a story.

- Activities 10 and 11 developed work around allowing exterior and interior locations to suggest narrative.
- You have been encouraged to think of the location as 'another character' – not just as a backdrop to the story, but as an active element in the drama that can affect and influence the course of the story.
- Earlier work in this chapter has given examples of how location can profoundly affect and change human behaviour – the London Underground

situation chosen by the Chickenshed group being an excellent example.

• In previous chapters, the use of objects received from the twin and placed in an abstract setting also began to create a sense of 'place'.

The following activity further develops the use of setting or location as a means of achieving greater integration of the shared creative work.

Activity 35 Sharing the setting

1 Decide with your twin to develop your plays using very similar locations.

2 Place a character or characters from your own culture in that of your twin (you may have already begun to do this in previous activities).

3 Take one of the characters being developed by your twin and place them in your own culture.

4 See if the developing narrative can move between your own cultural location and that of your twin.

5 See if very different locations have a 'feel' to them that resonates with the other – in terms of how they may impact on the story.

6 Review all the images sent to you by your twin group. Do any of them inspire an idea for the location of your story?

7 How far can you push the integration of your setting or location with that of your twin?

Example 35.1

Here are some examples of how different twinning projects were linked – in some way – by settings and locations that were similar, shared or have some resonance with each other:

1 *Rooftops at night*: A group of people on a city rooftop at night; one in Leeds, UK, and one in Damascus, Syria (Asian Theatre School, Bradford, and The Studio Theatre, Syria).

2 *The street as performance arena*:
   • 'A group of street artists, thrown together by fate and circumstance, arrive in a city, take over the space and weave a kind of anarchic magic on the inhabitants' (Young Blood, Leicester,UK).
   • 'The street as a circus ... where life itself is a great circus show' (Novos Novos, Teatro Villa Velha, Salvador, Brazil).

3 *Divided landscapes*:
   • 'A city divided by a river – two cultures divided by a common language (Act2LDN, UK).
   • 'Two factions on opposite sides of the fence – both scrambling to claim the turf' (Art of the Street, Grahamstown, South Africa).

4   Two images from our partner Akshen in Kuala Lumpur, Malaysia
        caught our imagination. A seat numbered 57, which we would later
        learn could be found inside the disused Merdeka Freedom Stadium
        in Kuala Lumpur, and a Wayang Kulit puppet used in the traditional
        shadow puppetry of the region. Our questions flowed thick and
        fast among ourselves and to our partners. What did we mean by
        freedom? Why seat 57? What was hiding in the shadows of that
        stadium? This all gave us the location for our story. It takes place
        within the walls of a ruined stadium, whose gates were locked many
        years ago . . . a place most people would like to forget.

                              (Live Theatre, Newcastle, UK, inspired by the
                                       images sent by Akshen, Malaysia)

Section six – theme

The theme or themes of a play are the 'big questions' that are at the heart of
any story. At some point in any process of creating new theatre, it is useful
– and perhaps crucial – to identify what our theme or themes are.

'Theme' is certainly linked to 'subject matter' – they are both what the
play is 'about'. But theme differs from subject matter in a crucial way.

- *Subject matter*. We have already looked at this earlier. It deals with an
  observable issue or topic: an area of human activity, behaviour, social
  concern or problem etc. – 'colonialism', 'leadership', 'social welfare',
  'ageism', 'fame', 'rural poverty', for example. All topics that can be
  somehow 'pinned down' and analysed from different angles, with possible
  solutions.
- *Theme*. This deals with questions that are less easy to solve: 'Are economic
  poverty and spiritual poverty one and the same?'; 'What is good leadership?'

We can find a solution to the issue of economic poverty (if we organised
ourselves in a decent and sensible way), but there is no easy solution to the
thematic question of the relativity of economic and spiritual poverty. This is
why 'theme' in a play can contribute to its complexity and interest. It is the
big question at the heart of the play.

So 'theme' is less easy to grasp than subject matter (topic, issue). But in
terms of the 'about' nature of the story you are making, I would encourage
you – at the appropriate stage in the process – to see if you can identify what
your theme or themes are. Not as an intellectual exercise, but in order to
identify what *major human concerns* might lie behind the story.

Don't worry if this doesn't come easily or immediately – though it might.
I recall working with two primary schools once – twinned with each other –
on a play they were making together. The play was going to be 'about' tribes,
gangs and conflict. One day I asked the children what they thought was

underneath the story – what great big questions about life the story was asking. One little girl wrote down something I will never forget. She wrote:

Is the future dark or is it full of light?

She had discovered a wonderful theme for the play, and, from that point on, as the twinned play was being made, I was able to refer back to it and ask the children if that question was being asked (in different ways) throughout the story. That is the practical use of discovering what the theme of the story is.

Activity 36 Finding the theme

1 Look through all the work you have done so far – particularly that based upon activities in this chapter – and make lists of what the theme or themes of the plays you are making are.

2 Choose one that seems nearest to the one major question (statement, observation) that may be at the heart of the story.

3 Share this with your twin. See what the similarities and differences between the themes are.

4 See if there might be one theme that both groups adopt.

5 Attempt to be as concise as possible. Remember the instance of the young pupil in the school.

Example 36.1

Here are some examples of themes that different groups involved in twinning projects have arrived at. Note how concise – though complex – they are.

- A man's life: what is it worth? Does another man exists only to the degree that he stands in your way? (Art of the Street, Grahamstown, South Africa)

- Can we know all the routes, but still lose our way? (Act2LDN, London, UK)

- What's the wrong place? In the wrong place for who? Is anything ever in the wrong place? Is everything in the wrong place? (IFAQ, Hope Street, Liverpool, UK)

- Control in everyday life – who has it, who wants it, who needs it, why do we deserve to have it? Where does control end and freedom begin? (Nine, Manchester, UK)

- When there is no hierarchy of importance, can there be equality of importance? (The Pandies, Delhi)

- What is the struggle and sense of ownership we feel – or allow others to feel – about where we come from? (Akshen, Kuala Lumpur, Malaysia)

Outcome

You have now begun to develop the outlines of the play you are making. If you have successfully incorporated creative material and inspirations from your twin, they should be able to hear echoes and see images from their own culture in the work – and vice versa. As one group put it, 'the boundaries between our characters seemed to dissolve . . . we were making completely new human beings out of our two different worlds'. Think of the two grandmothers in the story shared by the group from the UK and the group from Rwanda – how the key elements in their shared histories were a bottle of Scotch whisky and African groundnuts.

Some of your stories will be rooted in the specifics of your own culture, but you will also have found ways of weaving in the history, traditions and specifics of another culture.

From the examples in this chapter, you will have seen that the degrees in which this can happen can vary enormously – there is no 'set way' or formula to be followed. Indeed, it is often the small and seemingly inconsequential detail received from the twin that can inspire the beginnings of a whole story. Think of the empty seat in a ruined stadium in Malaysia that sparked the imaginations of a group in the UK and gave them a location for their story and questions that would feed that story.

You will have begun the twinning process with a 'game plan' – an agreed menu of exchanged activities and a time-schedule to work to. But the key is always to 'stay open' – to be prepared to incorporate and develop the exchange at all stages. The following chapters will look at aspects of how this may be achieved – although you will have also been advised to dip into these chapters already.

Cross-reference

See Activity 55.

Section seven – the big question

As I have said, at the heart of any story there is one large question that is being explored. It is something that is universal and relates to the human condition. It is generally never stated in the story, but is reflected in all the parts of it. It forms the basis of everything that is being explored in the story and lies at the heart of it.

The big question may be the same as your theme, but sometimes it is larger even that that. Think of it as being the very 'essence' of the play you are making. In English, 'essence' is defined as 'the fundamental nature' of something. What is the equivalent word in other languages? In Nigeria I discovered that one equivalent was '*Uhru*'. In Jordan it was '*Jahwer*'. In Brazilian, '*Essencia*'.

This 'essence' of a story can often best be expressed in a two-part question. It is something that cannot be answered by a simple 'yes' or 'no', but expresses a problem or dilemma that is never fully solved, but that is common to the lives of us all, no matter what our culture is.

Activity 37 Big questions in stories we know

Look at some stories you are familiar with, from your own culture or from other cultures. See if you can identify what the big question might be. There is no right or wrong here, and the group may come up with a range of possibilities.

Share what you have discovered with your twin. Read some of the stories they have used and see if you can come up with your own versions of what the big question might be.

Example 37.1

- Shakespeare's *Macbeth*: 'If we attempt to gain earthly power in this life, do we lose the right to spiritual salvation in the next life?'

- *Little Red Riding Hood*: 'In order fully to develop as an individual, how far do we need to rebel against the rules that we are told we must live by?'

- 'Is my loyalty shaped by my race, or by my sexuality?': many of the plays and novels by James Baldwin.

- *Macunaima*, by Mario de Andrade: 'How far do we need to journey in order to find where we wish to be?'

- *Antigone*, by Sophocles: 'When we take our life into our own hands, are we making the wisest decision?'

Activity 38 The big question in the story we are making

Think about the previous activity and its examples.

- See if you can identify the essence of the play you are making.

- Have a group buzz-session. Write lists of possible 'big questions'.

- *Exchange* lists with your twin group. Are there any similarities or significant differences in the questions you are both asking?

Section eight – mapping the play

Now might be the time to think about the 'map' of the play you are making. Chapter 8 will be looking at different story structures (and you may decide to dip into that chapter at this point). For the moment, take some time to think about the *journey of the play and the characters in it*. Remember that the story is always *going forward* (even if you intend to use flashback sequences). You can do this is any way, whichever is the most appropriate and enjoyable for the group.

Activity 39 The journey of the play

1   Use any of the following techniques to map the journey of the play. You might perhaps try dividing the group up and trying different ones. Each technique will shed different light on the same journey.

   Whatever techniques you use, you will be discovering exactly what the *key events* are in the story you are telling. Try and be as rigorous as possible. Keep *going forward* and don't get sidetracked into insignificant detail. Map the journey:

   •   as a list of 'things that happen along the way';
   •   as a literal 'map' on a large sheet of paper;
   •   as a series of postcards from the characters, saying what has just happened;
   •   as a sequence of photographs showing the key episodes in the journey (you can then use actual locations);
   •   as a newspaper report on the story (is it a straight news item, a piece of investigative journalism, a sensational story or interviews with one or more of the characters?);
   •   using any other techniques you can invent.

2   *Finally*, whatever techniques you have used, try and make a very brief 'boiled down' account of the story. If you can tell a complex story in one or two short paragraphs, you will know that you are on the right track – you will have a firm and clear idea about the 'what happens' of the story. Any good story – be it a great classic play or a simple folk tale, a linear narrative or an abstract one – should be able to be told in this manner. This is an excellent method to find out if you are being lazy in your thinking and avoiding making clear choices (see Example 39.1).

3   *Exchange* with your twin the story journeys you have depicted. Include the final 'boiled down' account. Are you satisfied that what you have sent your twin is as clear and uncluttered as possible? That they will be able to 'follow the map'?

4   Is what your twin has sent you clear? Have they led you clearly along the map?

5   See what the similarities and differences are.

6   See where the shared characters, locations etc. create similarities and differences.

7   See if the two play journeys can be brought even closer together.

8   Ask your twin a few significant questions about the journey of the play – questions that may prompt more new thoughts for them.

Example 39.1

Here are some examples of complex stories that can be boiled down to an essence of 'what happens'. By 'complex', I mean that even a relatively simple folk or fairy tale such as *Little Red Riding Hood* can be as deep as a classic play in terms of human experience.

*   Shakespeare's *Macbeth*: An ambitious general is rewarded for his bravery and loyalty by his king. Encouraged by the prophecies of glory from three witches and the ambitions of his wife, he adopts violent means to become king himself and, in so doing, ruins his reputation and his sense of self worth.

*   *Little Red Riding Hood*: A young girl is instructed by her mother to visit her grandmother and stay safely on the path through the woods. She decides to please herself by picking flowers, which leads her off the path, and in so doing she meets a hungry wolf and is confronted by, and finally survives, all the dangers that life can bring.

*   *Macunaima*, by Mario de Andrede: Making the journey away from his birthplace in search of a precious object he has lost, Macunaima gratifies all his material and sexual desires along the way. Surviving many changes of fortune and physical shape, he finds that he has lost both his home and his way in the world and decides to go up to the heavens and live in the stars.

*   *Antigone*, by Sophocles: Antigone's brother has rebelled against the king, has been executed and is not allowed a legal burial. His sister defies the law and, in burying her brother, embraces her own death, despite the opportunity to save herself.

Outcome

You have begun to get a solid idea of what your play is about. 'About' both in terms of the 'what happens', in the story and to the characters, and what lies *beneath* the story in terms of its themes and the major questions it is asking. You have begun to give the play its structure.

Cross-reference

See Chapter 8.

Section nine – checking the connections

Now might be a useful stage in the process to remind yourselves of the connections between the play you are making and the one your twin is making.

All the activities have been about creating material for the plays through the process of exchange. You have found that the unexpected and the accidental can be as inspiring as the expected and the planned for. Things that have at first seemed problematic have become opportunities. The 'mantra' is that *everything is there to be used.*

What are the key points of creative connection in the work? Where does the work you are making overlap with that of your twin group?

Activity 40 Key connections

1   Make a list of those major elements in your play directly inspired by what your twin group has given you. This can include:

   • *images and objects*: ones that you received from your twin that play a central part in the story you are telling;
   • *characters*: ones that you have been given by your twin, or who have characteristics and histories drawn from the culture of your twin;
   • *language*: words or phrases from the language culture of your twin that you have incorporated into your play;
   • *location(s)*: places that the story is set in that draw upon those suggested by your twin;
   • *narrative(s)*: episodes, scenes or events in your story that have been suggested by things your twin has told you;
   • *issues, topics and themes*: ones that have been suggested to you by your twin.

2   Look at the list your twin has sent you.

   • What things from the above list do you share?
   • Which things could be shared even more – characters, scenes, themes etc.?
   • How far could you push the possibility of 'one whole play made together'?

Activity 41 Summing up the story

At every point in the process, it is useful to find ways of summing up the story you are creating: to find the 'essence' of it. You have already begun to look at this through some of the previous activities in this chapter. Now is the time to remember that you are making something for the public. You need to 'sell' your play – and to do it in a way that represents it fairly and honestly. This activity will give you another method of establishing just what your play is about.

1   Imagine that you are a member of the public. You are looking through a range of flyers that advertise performances of new plays. You will go to the one that seems to offer you something you've not seen before, in terms of what it is going to be about.

2   Now imagine that you are the person writing the copy for the flyer that is going to get the attention of that member of the public – the one advertising your play. Your task is to get across an essence of the story to the stranger who knows nothing about your group or the process you have been involved in. What might that be? Make lists of possibilities. Choose the one that you think will 'grab' the person in the street and get them to come and see your play. The key thing to remember is – be brief, be specific and be as honest as you can be as to what you are offering that stranger. Arouse their curiosity. Be warned – phrases such as 'A great night out' or 'The best show in town' are very overused and tired and won't have very much effect! (See Example 41.1.)

3   *Exchange* your example with your twin. Do the two examples resonate with each other? Do they give a sense of two plays that have something in common?

4   If you are happy with the results, the members of the group responsible for publicity and advertising will have something to work with!

Example 41.1

Here are some examples of brief summaries of plays, devised by companies that have been involved in twinning projects. All of them could be suitable as copy for flyers, and all of them give an essence of the plays that were made.

- 'Does the best food in the world satisfy the deepest hunger in our hearts?'
- 'Do we only appreciate what we have when we leave it behind?'
- 'Intellectuals are killed and driven out. Can a culture keep growing if it loses its thinkers?'
- 'Why do people take and sell drugs?'
- 'We want to know what you are thinking. If you don't know . . . we'll tell you soon enough!'
- 'The play digs deep into the MUD of the human spirit, to see how we can survive in a digitalized world'.

Cross-reference

See Activity 47.

Outcome

You have now identified just how much you have been inspired by the work your twin has offered you, and how much of it has fed into the narrative you are making. You can now decide if you would like to go even further down the path of creating two plays that 'interlock' and resonate with each other. The process of adapting the work can go on right up to the final moments of rehearsals.

COMMENT – ON ASPECTS OF WORK IN THIS CHAPTER

We adopted the character of a street performer in the UK . . . in Brazil the buskers range from being funny to being politically minded. We decided that the street performers we created could do anything with confidence, that we could be the best acrobats even if that meant we were standing on one foot. Also, both plays had angels . . . by chance, both companies had read a story about 'a very old man with very enormous wings', which became an image in both productions.

(Young Blood, UK)

We decided with our twin to create 'one mind' regarding the work of taxi drivers in the UK and South Africa. In South Africa, we first thought that taxi drivers would be corrupt street men, then after interviews we discovered many of them were family churchgoers. By conducting the interviews with taxi drivers, we were able to find more about our own community.

(Art of the Street, South Africa)

The call centre theme we shared was really appropriate to us both. Lots of call centres were being transferred to India for cheaper labour. Here in Manchester we'd got this brand new call centre building that didn't give jobs, as they'd all gone to India.

(Company member, Contact, UK)

The subject of our play was war and slavery, to let the world know how lives are affected in our area. There is a war between Muslims and Christians, with threats of bombings and kidnapping. It is dubbed 'the training ground for terrorism' around the world, and now people fear to go there. Theatre helps people to open their minds against what the media projects.

(Sining Kambayoka Ensemble, Philippines)

5   Working methods

Through all the work you have done so far, you will have been developing
your own working methods and engaging with those of your twin group. By
'working methods' I mean:

- the ways in which you organise your work;
- the ways in which you develop your work;
- the ways in which 'leadership' operates in your group;
- the schedules you work to;
- the ways in which you assess the outcomes of your work.

It may be that your twin group has very different working methods to your
own. You will already have found ways to negotiate those differences, and
perhaps you have begun to incorporate into your own practices some new
ways of working inspired by your twin. Previous chapters have given examples
of how this can happen. In this chapter, we will be looking at how you might
go even further outside the 'comfort zone' of your own working methods and
practices. Some of the advice and guidance given here will be familiar, but it
is worth reminding ourselves of the key points, since the *exchange of working
methods* is as crucial to the project as the *exchange of creative material*. The
chapter will therefore focus on the following:

- *Leadership*. What is good leadership? Where does 'leadership' become
  'control'? Are there different cultural responses to the notion of leadership? Is leadership something that can be learned?
- *Collaboration*. What do we mean by 'collaboration'? Are there different
  cultural interpretations of what it means?
- *The unexpected*. In a process, how can we stay open to the idea of 'the
  unexpected'? How can we embrace new and unfamiliar ways of working?

- *The accidental.* How do we keep alert to the possibility that something that *seems* not 'to fit' with what was planned or prepared for can be embraced?
- *Failure and disappointment.* When presented with new ways of working, how do we deal with the sense that we have 'failed to grasp' something (a technique or a way of organising our work) offered by the twin group? How do we deal with the fact that the twin group has not fully grasped what you have offered them?

Section one – why and how do you make theatre?

It is always useful to think about why we do something and how we do it. In the case of a creative exchange project this assumes an even greater importance – particularly because the process will challenge and develop both the *why* and the *how*.

Activity 42 The how and the why

1   Make a list of points that make your group unique. Include as many of the points below as are useful or appropriate. There may be as many answers to each question as there are people in the group. See if there are one or two answers to each question that – in some way – seem to include all the other answers. Add other questions of your own to the list.

- Why do we make theatre?
- How long have we been working as a group?
- What kind of space(s) do we work in?
- Who leads and why?
- How do time and scheduling operate in a typical workshop or creative session?
- What do we focus on normally – physical, vocal, textual or visual work?
- What methods and techniques do we use?
- Do we work as a whole group, or do we work in small groups?
- Why should people want to become involved with our work?
- What kinds of story do we believe need to be told?
- Does our work relate to any particular issues?
- Do we have our own artistic style?
- What does 'success' mean for our group?
- What does 'failure' mean to our group?
- How do individual participants make our theatre what it is?

2   Once you have formed your ideas, create a short performance that expresses some or all of the above. Keep it short (think of it as a 'mini-play'). Make it any style you wish. Make a record of the performance – as text, film or photographs.

3   *Exchange* with your twin the mini-play and the lists you have come up with.

Outcome

•   By examining why and how you make theatre, you have given your twin an insight into your creative processes as they exist. You have gained an insight into the creative processes of your twin. Now you can both be prepared to borrow from each other's working processes.

•   By developing the research into your working methods as a mini-play, you have 'shown' as well as 'told'. What might have been a rather dry list has become another creative output. Once again, we see that *anything* can be inspiration for creativity.

Section two – leadership

Whenever I have been responsible for leading a group – as play director, tutor or facilitator – I have noticed something that is crucial to whether or not I can do my job to the best of my abilities. It is something that is completely unrelated to what I bring – good, bad or indifferent – to the process. And that is the 'internal leadership' within the group.

Any group has its own dynamic, and central to this is the internal leadership that exists within the group. This is something that the 'official leader' may not be aware of – particularly if it is a group that is new to her or him. We can find ourselves working in a familiar situation – with a year group in a known school or a college, say – and find that *this year's group* is negative, unfocussed and rebellious, whereas *last year's group* was positive, focussed and co-operative.

Of course, it is always clear which are 'the loud mouths' or the 'shy ones', and we adopt strategies for working with them. But there is often something less obvious and tangible going on beneath the surface of the group, something possibly not even acknowledged or articulated. 'The loud mouth' may take up more air time, 'the shy one' may seem to have little to contribute, but that does not necessarily indicate where the internal leadership in the group lies. I have sometimes finished a project and said, 'that went well, what a great group that was to work with'. Other times I have said, 'that went really badly, that was a very difficult group to work with'. A lot of the responsibility for that is, of course, my own, even though I have offered to both groups the same things. But, in hindsight, I have also recognised that an internal dynamic within a group – something outside my control – has seriously affected the way the group operates. If there is 'good' internal leadership, then the way has been paved for me to do my work well. The 'bad' internal leadership can create blocks and divisions that disrupt the work.

So, in our work, it is worth spending some time – at the very outset of a project maybe – thinking about ways in which to address the notion of leadership, how it operates and how good leadership can be encouraged. In this way, we can hopefully address creatively the particular dynamic that a group brings into the room with it, and not have to rely on hindsight to tell us what that was. There will be some activities suggested below. But before that, it can be useful to establish some ground rules that everyone in the group agrees to, as a basis for any working methods adopted. Here are a few I have found useful, but you will discover others:

- *'Yes'*, *'And'*, *'But'*, *'No'* and *'Because'*. In a group, we earn the right to say 'no' to an idea, a suggestion or a thought only if we have begun with the 'yes'. The bad leader in a group will always begin with the 'no' – a negative response to, or dismissal of, what someone else has said or suggested. The tendency to say 'no' can spread like wildfire. It is a very easy option – it protects us from taking risks, from considering the new, from reflecting on the unfamiliar. It can be very comforting to say 'no'. To say 'yes' can be to open out and be responsive, to take risks.

  Once we are in the habit of saying 'yes' ('Yes, let's try that idea out'), then we can add the 'and' ('Yes, let's try that idea out and perhaps we could also bring this other idea into it'). Then we have earned the right to bring in the 'but' ('That was a great idea, but it might work better this time if we did this . . .'). 'No' comes last, and should always be treated with caution, but it does have its place. 'No, I don't think we should do it like that, because . . .' And, of course, 'because' is perhaps the most important word because there is a thoughtfulness behind it.
- *Equal 'air time' for all.* In any group discussion or activity, everyone should have the equal opportunity to have as much space ('air time') to put forward their ideas, thoughts or feelings. 'Don't hog the microphone' is a catchphrase one group I worked with used.
- *Report-backs.* Everyone in the group has the responsibility during the process to report back on aspects of the work.
- *Everyone can be a leader.* Everyone in the group has the equal right and responsibility to take on the role of leader. Everyone in the group will support each other in this (remembering always the 'yes', 'and', 'but', 'no' and 'because . . .').

Activity 43 Everyone can be a leader

As a group, you are going to explore different approaches to leadership. Try these options:

1   Undertake a theatre-making activity that you are *familiar with*, making sure that *everyone has an equal role*.

2   Undertake a theatre-making activity that is *new to you*, making sure that *everyone has an equal role*.

3   Undertake a theatre-making activity in which *someone leads*, but in which *everyone has an equal role*. Make sure that *everyone* in the group has a chance at this.

4   Undertake a theatre-making activity in which *no-one leads*, and *no words or physical contact are involved.*

5   Undertake a theatre-making activity in which *the leader changes throughout*. Make sure that *everyone* in the group has a chance at this.

6   Feed back to your twin group the activities you undertook.

7   Receive the activities your twin undertook.

8   Try out the activities your twin sent you.

Outcome

You will have explored different methods of leadership. Everyone in the group will have had the experience of 'being leader'. You will have discovered how your twin group responds to the idea of leadership in a practical way. Think about the following:

•   Did the activities come easily?

•   What were the problems?

•   What new things occurred?

•   How successful was your group in using your twin group's activities?

•   What aspects of the activities best demonstrated the meaning of 'leading', 'working together' and 'collaborating'?

Section three – collaboration

In Chapter 2 we looked at some collaborative activities, both theatre- and non-theatre based. Chapter 3 developed the collaborative process. It is now worth reminding ourselves – as the plays begin to evolve and take shape – of the importance of keeping our shared working methods open to the possibilities of collaboration.

The word 'collaboration' itself could be looked at. We have considered the challenges of translation, and how a word in one language might have very different meanings and nuances in another. The very term 'collaborative process', as used in English in this book, may – when translated into languages that do not have a basis in Latin or German (two of the roots of the English language) – have very different meanings. It might be useful to share with the twin group just what you both mean by the word, and what it implies in terms of how you work.

Activity 44 What is 'collaboration'?

1   Write a list of words or phrases you associate with the word 'collaborate' (in English, if that is your first language, or in your own first language if it is not English). (See Example 44.1.)

2   What is a dictionary definition of the word 'collaborate' in your first language? (See Example 44.2.)

3   *Exchange* your findings with your twin group. What differences in meaning or nuance exist between your uses of the word? (See Example 44.3).

Example 44.1

(English) Collaborate: to work together, to work as a team, to pool resources, to join in, interact, team work, share, to pull together etc.

Example 44.2

(English) Collaborate. From Latin, *collaborare*: *com* – together + *laborare* – to work. 'To work with one another or others on a joint project'. 'To co-operate as a traitor, especially with an enemy occupying one's own country'.

Example 44.3

Here we have an interesting lesson in what 'translation' means. A colleague of mine who comes from a Hindi-speaking culture had this to say:

> There is no equivalent word for 'collaborate' in the Hindi language. When I asked friends and family if there was one, they replied by asking 'What is the context?' Of course you need a context, but in this case all I was asking for was the Hindi equivalent of the word collaborate. I myself had slightly presumed there would have been a direct equivalent but there wasn't. I then had to search around to find the closest words or phrases that would match the word collaborate. The action of the word 'collaborate' in its simplest form is 'to work together'. I naturally thought then that the Hindi phrase for the word 'collaborate' would definitely include the Hindi word '*kama*', which is 'work'. I presumed too much. The most formal was of saying 'collaborate' in Hindi includes the word '*kArya*'.
>
> To get the idea across of 'collaborate', there are many phrases that you can use, each with their own subtleties. Below are three examples. The capital letters should be stressed more when pronounced.
>
> 1   '*eka sAtha kArya karanA*': this phrase says 'to work together' and is put in the purest, formal form of Hindi;

2   'ahum sub milke hAma kare';
3   'eka sAtha milke kAma kare'.

Phrases 1 and 2 also say 'to work together', but are put in less formal terms.

The most important detail to remember is to never presume that there will be an instant translation. If you translate the idea, then you might get a quicker response from the group you are working with, and you might then find a better expression or phrase to get your idea across.

(Amit Sharma)

Outcome

With this very simple activity – looking at a word that is at the heart of the process – we have learned not to assume that what we mean by a word is what other cultures mean by it. Amit's advice is something we should bear in mind when dealing with different languages in our creative work together.

When looking at the various meanings of words in our own language, there is also much to be gained. To look beneath the usual use of a word can open up all kinds of interesting creative thoughts and possibilities. The example of an English meaning of 'collaborate' being 'To co-operate as a traitor' is particularly interesting – a whole other way of looking at the word. Indeed, here is a great example of 'the accidental or unexpected' offering creative opportunities – how about a play created through a collaborative ('working together') process being about a group of collaborative traitors?

The 'accidental and the unexpected' are indeed things that will occur during the process. And they are not to be ignored. They can provide great opportunities.

Section four – the unexpected, the accidental, failure and disappointment

In Chapter 9 you will find reference to the philosophy and practice of the playing of gamelan music. One of the great teachers said that there was 'no right or wrong, only good or bad'. 'Good' and 'bad' are loaded words – implying 'success' or 'failure'. But he was talking in the context of people working together, and I think we may safely take it that what he meant is: there is the *helpful or the not helpful*.

So, in the process you are involved with, you may feel at times that you have 'failed' at a task (or that your twin group has 'failed you'). You may have a sense of disappointment at times. But always keep in mind that *there is no failure, there is only the attempt to be helpful*.

I have mentioned the importance of taking on board the unexpected and the accidental in the creative work – how a seemingly unimportant detail, or the diversion from the expected outcome of an activity may be the key to some exciting new avenue ('collaborators can be traitors', for example).

So too, in the sharing of working methods, your twin may send you an idea that, at first, seems unimportant, but that opens up new paths for you to follow. They may seem odd or insignificant. Try them.

Activity 45 Different ways of working

1   Make a record of different techniques or methods you have used in your process. They may be ones you use regularly, or ones you have invented on the spur of the moment to help you. Send these to your twin group.

2   Receive your twin's record. Adapt some of the methods they have used, or keep them in mind as some of the options you have for your own working methods.

Example 45.1

Here are some examples of ways of working that different groups have used to approach an activity, or to get them over a particular difficulty in the process:

*   'We didn't know how to get to the heart of the scene, so we danced it out.'
*   'We weren't happy with the dialogue we came up with – it was boring – so we invented a made-up language and it came alive.'
*   'We felt the devised scene was all over the place, so two of us who were interested in writing were elected to go away and script it.'
*   'We have been working without a director, and that has been good. But now that we are putting the whole play together, we have decided to bring in a director for the final rehearsals. So we are in the unusual position of actors employing a director!'
*   'We felt the play was being trapped inside the rehearsal room, so we took the whole thing out to the beach and did it there. The sky and the sea liberated it.'
*   'We asked the director of the play to not come to the next session.'
*   'We used the mask-activity and decided to perform the whole play in masks.'
*   'We couldn't agree on the best ending, so we agreed to have three different endings.'
*   'We always begin our rehearsals with a group discussion about the scene we are about to do.'
*   'We always write scenes and speeches for *each other*. We never speak the words that we have written.'
*   'We always make sure that we have some sign-language in the play, so that people in the audience who cannot hear know what is being said.'

- 'We always improvise, and never come up with a set script. We know what is meant to happen in the scene, but it is always different, even in the performances.'

Outcome

Your twin group may have sent you some suggestions for ways of working that are very unfamiliar to you – indeed perhaps alarming. Be bold, use and adapt them, see if they open creative doors for you. Throwing away the safety of the script (if this is how you usually work) and improvising the play could be liberating. 'Dancing the scene out' could give it new life. Taking the play to the seashore could give it a whole new dimension.

The ability to adapt to new working methods is as important as the ability to embrace new creative activities: they work together. With both, you will discover that:

> We are not who we expected ourselves to be.
> You are not who we expected you to be.

COMMENT – ASPECTS OF WORK IN THIS CHAPTER

> Our ways of working were very different. We – here in our UK group – have an idea then get up and just start doing something. Our Indian group sits down and talks for a long time before they actually start doing something. We learned from each other's ways of getting started, and both brought those things into our ways of working.
>
> (Company member, Contact, UK)

> We now incorporate more movement in our pieces. We are now more aware of space as a group.
>
> (Cumbernauld Youth Theatre, Scotland, UK)

> Our twin is a group that is strong with their physicality, testing bodies like elastic rubber. We learned how to flex our bodies, make shapes to move into emotions, sentences and phrases. They base a lot of their work on images, which we have adopted.
>
> (Phakama, India)

> The project allowed myself and the other artists to acknowledge a theatre practice that went beyond a Western European understanding of theatre – a practice that was informed by a culture and history beyond the shores of the UK.
>
> (Madani Younis, Asian Theatre School, UK)

> We made a phone call to our twin just before we started rehearsals, to check in with them and to focus ourselves through the immediate contact with them.
>
> (Company member, Contact, UK)

The question of adapting to your twin's working methods should take on board the differences – and inequalities – of access to technologies.

> The instruments used – the English language and the internet – are not fairly distributed and accessible to people living in different places, thus hampering an equal exchange or, worse, excluding large groups of potential participants. In our case, our young people had just started on learning some English, and I was the only person with access to the internet (located at a distance). Being based in a rural area, we have no access to the internet . . . therefore the entire exchange had to be mediated through an adult – something which took away a lot of the directness and of the 'peer-feeling' of the process.'
>
> (Kattaikuttu Sangam, India)

Plate 1 Street Performance, *Contacting the World* 2006.
Photo credit: Mario Popham

Plate 2 Workshop, *Contacting the World* 2006.
Photo credit: Mario Popham

Plate 3 Workshop, *Contacting the World* 2006.
Photo credit: Mario Popham

Plate 4 Workshop, *Contacting the World* 2006.
Photo credit: Mario Popham

Plate 5 Carnival performance rehearsal, *Contacting the World* 2006.
Photo credit: Mario Popham

Plate 6 Street Performance, *Contacting the World* 2006.
Photo credit: Mario Popham

Plate 7 Street Performance, *Contacting the World* 2006.
Photo credit: Mario Popham

Plate 8 Contact's foyer Street Performance, *Contacting the World* 2006.
Photo credit: Mario Popham

Plate 9 Noël Greig & *CTW* team meeting, *Contacting the World* 2006.
Photo credit: Mario Popham

Plate 10 Performance by Sining Kambayoka Ensemble (The Philippines), *Contacting the World* 2006.
Photo credit: Mario Popham

Plate 11 Performance by Nine (Manchester), *Contacting the World* 2006.
Photo credit: Mario Popham

Plate 12 Performance by Mashirika (Rwanda), *Contacting the World* 2006.
Photo credit: Mario Popham

Plate 13 Performance by Macrobert (Scotland), *Contacting the World* 2006.
Photo credit: Mario Popham

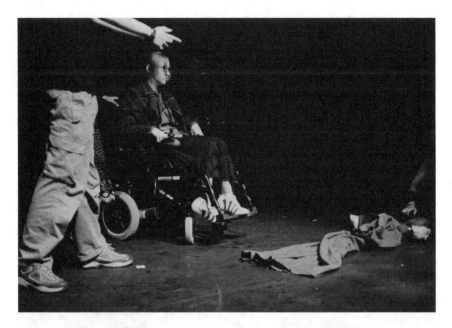

Plate 14 Performance by Macrobert (Scotland), *Contacting the World* 2006.
Photo credit: Mario Popham

Plate 15 Performance by Massive Theatre (New Zealand), *Contacting the World* 2006.
Photo credit: Mario Popham

Plate 16 Warm up workshop, *Contacting the World* 2006.
Photo credit: Mario Popham

Plate 17 Carnival workshop, *Contacting the World* 2006.
Photo credit: Mario Popham

Plate 18 Workshop by Art of the Street (Anisa), *Contacting the World* 2006.
Photo credit: Mario Popham

Plate 19 Workshop, *Contacting the World* 2006.
Photo credit: Mario Popham

Plate 20 Professional Development workshop, *Contacting the World* 2006.
Photo credit: Mario Popham

6 Full participation

It has already been made clear that everyone should contribute to the creative work, and many of the activities have suggested different approaches to encouraging this. This is the heart of the project. But this should not rule out the importance of individuals – or small teams – engaging with other aspects of the project. The notion of 'full ownership' should extend into adjacent *specific theatre skill areas*, and the *structural* and *organisational* work that goes into the project. This is not simply about the ethos and practice of the project, though. It is about the future horizons that the project may open up for its participants.

Theatre is an industry. Some of us involved in it might fight shy of the word – it carries meanings that conflict with other words: 'creativity', 'imagination', 'expression' etc. But in the range of skills-development it offers – beyond the obvious one of the development of performing talent – it encompasses a huge range of possibilities. The full participation of the group in all aspects of the creative project is essential to its ethos, but the full value of that participation can extend far beyond its particular lifetime into the economic future and well-being of its members.

I was reminded of this very forcefully just recently, having just returned from a working visit to Brazil. While I was there I spent some time in one of the poorer areas of Rio. They are called *favelas*, and the English translation is 'slum' or 'shanty town' (in India such areas are called *bastis*, and a South African version might be 'township'). Anyway, the *favelas* are where the economically deprived and socially abandoned make their lives. In the *favela* I visited is a theatre company called Nos do Morro ('Us from the Hillside').

It was a place teeming with life and creativity, of an order that one would be hard-pressed to find in the UK. In my brief time there I asked some of the people what they regarded as the purposes of the work being done. In one sense I had no need to ask – the energy and creative life that was evident throughout the place gave the immediate answer. 'Well', said one of the tutors (a young man who had found the theatre company when he was a child, and who had grown up in it) 'some us go on to earn our livings outside the *favela*, as actors and dancers. But this is not a place for "making Hollywood stars". It also equips young people with all sorts of skills that may earn them a living later on in life. Ways of earning a living that may save them from the guns and the drugs'. He went on to talk about how the involvement in 'theatre' – in all of its aspects – is not just about 'being creative', but has a very practical outcome. He was not talking theory. He was talking about a type of shared, creative human activity that could save lives from guns and drugs. There was nothing sentimental in what he was saying. And it put into a sharp perspective the comments one hears from time to time that 'the arts' are somehow above and beyond the grubby details of economics and industry.

The projects encouraged by this book, or many of the ones referred to, may not be on such an extreme edge as the work being done in that *favela* in Rio. But I would like to suggest that the 'full participation' of your own group might bear some relation to the insights into the 'function of art' expressed by the young man from Nos do Morro.

So, looking beyond the immediate value of a creative, intercultural exchange, with all the life-learning benefits it brings, let us consider the future working lives of the participants and the widening of their opportunities for employment that has meaning and pleasure.

Here are some ways in which participants can develop those skills – not only ensuring that the group has access to all aspects of the project, but also equipping them with expertise and confidence for possible future employment.

Section one – specific theatre skills

Although everyone should contribute equally to the creative process, the doors should be open for individuals or small teams to engage with specific skills that are adjacent to the 'literary' aspect of the making of the play (the development of the story), but that are essential to its final success.

Activity 46 Adjacent skills

1   *Set design and making*:
   - Read a play or a story. Make drawings of different ways you would create a stage setting for it.
   - Make small, three-dimensional models of how you make a practical stage setting from the drawings.
   - Find books with illustrations of set designs. Look at ways in which seemingly difficult things can be represented on stage – how to show a mountain top without actually building one, how to suggest a city without actually constructing one, how to represent a working kitchen without using a real cooker and a real fridge, for example.

There was a theatre company in America called The Cardboard Box Players. They had very little money when they started out, and all their sets were made from cardboard and paper they found in rubbish skips in the streets. Their sets were equal in imagination to any of the more luxurious ones seen on Broadway.

- Take a scene from the play the group is making and create an environment for it. Try the scene again within this environment.
- Look at the whole play that is being made. Make drawings or models of different ways in which one simple stage setting could incorporate all the different scenes.
- Think about the space you will be performing the play in. If it is a conventional theatre, you will need ground plans and dimensions, so that your set will fit into it. If you are using a non-theatre space you may find that much of your design is already there for you, and that you need only a few things to transform it. (A friend of mine, who is an experienced set designer, said that, 'All we needed to do, in order to turn the park into a magic space, was to tie ribbons round the trees').
- If you are going to take your play to another part of the country – or to a different country – bear in mind just how much you will be able to transport. (A friend of mine, who is a set designer, said, 'I always start thinking about the size of the van before I begin to design the set').
- Find someone who works as a set designer. Show them the work you have done. Get them to show you examples of their work. What are the 'tricks of the trade'? What is the difference between a 'realistic' set and an abstract design? Which suits your play best? What is *the least* you can manage with to create the best setting for your play? Consult a carpenter, or other 'makers'. Are your designs practical?
- *Make a budget.* How much will the set cost? This is perhaps as important as anything else. It is no use planning for ten set changes when your project can only afford two chairs! If it is two chairs, which are the *right* two chairs? (I have often seen plays done with two chairs, used imaginatively, that have worked more effectively than those done with massive sets).
- *Recycle!* Use as many found objects and materials as you can.
- *Exchange* any of the above work with your twin. Incorporate their ideas into your own work. You may have already used items from the box in Chapter 2 as key props. How might your own full set designs reflect the influences of another culture?

2   *Lighting and sound design*:
- As with the set design, think about the different ways you can enhance the play through the use of lighting and sound technologies. Consult people who have worked in these areas. What is the scope

of your ambition, and what can be achieved most effectively within your budgets? (I have seen plays that have been lit solely by hand-held torches, and this has been just as effective as others lit by hundreds of lamps. The use of a simple repeating sound or chord can be just as effective as a huge variety of sounds.)

- *Exchange* your thoughts with your twin. Incorporate their ideas into your own work.

3   *Costume design and making*:

- Once again, explore all the different possibilities for creating a unique 'look' for the play. Remember that even the most 'realistic' setting for the play (daily life in the town or the village, for example) may be represented through costume that is not *exactly* as it might be in 'real life'. (I remember seeing a play set in a 'real' house, where everyone wore 'real' clothes, but all of them were in shades of blue). Draw on the skills of people you know who make clothes. Rummage through the second-hand clothes shops.
- *Exchange* your ideas with your twin. Incorporate their ideas into your own work.

4   *Prop design and making*:

- Every object on the stage tells a story, however small and insignifi-cant. Some may be 'found' items, some will need to be specially made. But in all cases, the care in the selection or the making should be equal to that taken with the whole set design. With the 'made props', great ingenuity and skill are often needed, and it is a craft that is highly valued in the theatre industry. (One play I saw, set in a 'realistic' house, had all the props – teacups, televisions, plates and bowls of flowers etc. – as beautifully made, two-dimensional cardboard cut-outs.)
- *Exchange* your ideas with your twin. Have any of the props you are making or finding been influenced by the culture of your twin? Have significant objects or images sent by your twin become key features in what things are used in the play?

Outcome

By involving members of the team in all of the above, we have:

- ensured that all the skills supporting the play and the performers are open to anyone in the group; the full participation in all aspects of bringing the play to its audience has been in the hands of the group – quite literally;
- seen that the *most effective* application of those skills is about what is *most appropriate* to the play that is being made; and that what is appropriate may not need to be the most lavish or expensive way

forward (think about the Cardboard Box Players, or the play lit by hand-held torches);

- related the imaginative ambition to the budgets and resources to hand;
- involved the collaboration of experienced practitioners, but not as 'experts' imported to make the decisions, more as enthusiastic supporters and guides;
- opened the door to possible work opportunities for the future;
- discovered new ways of incorporating the visual and sound worlds of your twin group into your own work.

Section two – structural and organisational skills

Other 'behind the scenes' skills should also be open to the full participation of the group: individuals or small teams who have an interest in the management of a project.

Activity 47 More adjacent skills

- *Planning and scheduling.* There will be people in the group who have a natural gift for 'making plans'. Draw them into the forward-planning aspect of the project. The successful outcome of a creative project can hinge on efficient management as much as the artistic process. Encourage the habit of always bringing 'management' decisions back to the whole group. In the 'theatre industry' (as in any other), there is often an unhelpful distance between the 'managers' and the 'artists'. There may well be people in the group who later go on to make working lives in the field of arts administration. The experience of the collaboration between management and artists will be invaluable.

  The development of a clear, agreed schedule between the twin groups will be one essential aspect of the work of any management team.

- *Marketing and advertising.* There will be people in the group who have a natural gift for graphics, poster design, leaflet and programme design and layout etc. Encourage those skills to develop to the full. Bring in the advice and expertise of local people who work in these fields.

- *A steering group.* A small team that meets regularly to discuss all aspects of the project and its development can be of great value. This can include people who are not necessarily involved in the play, but have an interest in it, and may have good advice and questions as 'outside eyes'. The involvement of the wider community at this point can be invaluable.

- *Budgeting.* This has already been mentioned – how creative decisions about sets, costumes etc. cannot be divorced from hard economic facts. There will be people in the group who have a natural gift for mathematics and the use of financial resources. Use and develop those skills.

- *Stage management.* The stage managers of a production are often the key element to its success, and good stage managers are 'gold dust'. They combine an ability to deal with the precision of getting the play and the players ready to begin the performance on the dot with that to deal with a last-minute crisis. They have a gift for efficient time-management combined with an understanding of human nature. Too often the role of stage manager is underestimated. There will be people in the group who do not elect to perform, but who have a natural interest in this 'backstage' role. Anyone in the group with such an interest should be encouraged and fully valued from the start of the project.

- An exchange of ideas and thoughts between the twin groups regarding all or any of the above can add to the richness of the project.

Outcome

By fully involving members of the group in all aspects of the project, you will have given full ownership to its members. You will have also demonstrated that the making of theatre is indeed a collaborative process that involves a huge range of skills: the ones the public sees and all the others that feed into a successful result. The person who does the sums is as important as the star of the show; the team that makes the costumes is as valuable as the cast that takes the final bow; the layout of the programme is as essential as the script.

COMMENT – ASPECTS OF WORK IN THE CHAPTER

If you are working without a director, as we did, don't feel it is wrong to bring one in at the very end of the process, to help put everything into its final place.

(Company member, Contact, UK)

There was no divide between us, like 'we are adults and you are teen-agers'. All were on the same wavelength. We spent a long time in making decisions together, to have an equal input regarding the set, costumes and direction of the play.

(Company member, Young Blood, UK)

The external director was forced on us at the end of the process. If you are going to have an adult to be part of the process, then they have to start at the beginning. It could have been helpful to have a dramaturge work with us. Also, there aren't enough young people being trained as directors.

(Company member, Contact, UK)

7 Form and style

It will be clear by now that the exchange process is about the genuine fusion of work: the creation of the new and the unique out of the collaboration of differences. You have been encouraged to stay as open as possible – for as long as possible – to all the opportunities that new inspirations from your twin group have offered. However, at a certain point along the way, the plays you are making will begin to take definite shape. You will have discovered the characters and their journeys, the general outline of the narrative, and the themes and issues that underpin the narrative. Soon, decisions will have to be made about the *crafting* of all this work into a coherent whole – something that will engage an audience for a specific period of time, with its own unique method of presentation. This chapter, and the following one, will offer some thoughts on how you might approach this.

First though, it is worth reminding ourselves of the challenges of the whole project. Even as we approach the final stages of making the play, we should not lose sight of them: there should never be a point where we say 'Alright, we've "done the process", now let's get on with the real work'. The real work *is* the process, and its key challenges are:

- to push the 'fusion' as far as possible by fully embracing the creative gifts offered by the twin group;
- to select from what is offered as genuinely creative inputs into our own work;
- to not reduce the inputs of the twin group to cosmetic 'add-ons';
- to resist the easy option of returning to the safety of known ways of working;
- to stay open to the unexpected, the new and the different right up to 'the finishing line'.

The activities in this chapter and in Chapter 8 will look at some ways in which the final shape of the play, and how it is presented, can be approached.

It will look at how this can happen alongside the continued fusion of work between the groups. Many of the activities in the preceding chapters (particularly Chapter 5) will have prepared the ground for this work.

Activity 48 Fully embracing other cultures

These days – in our globalised world – we are used to seeing images of particular cultural forms and styles of performance. As 'tourists' we may have been invited to witness displays of 'traditional culture'. I have seen English morris dancers in Trafalgar Square performing for the camera-carrying crowds, and Indonesian mask-theatre in Bali presenting their work to similar snap-happy hordes. Such events are generally 'heritage reproductions' intended for the tourist industry – culture cut off from its roots and re-presented as spectacle for the consumer.

The promotion of 'traditional' culture by the establishment can also be seen as the attempt to peddle a view of history and social relations that is convenient for the establishment. In the UK, the 'heritage industry' promotes the 'English country house' (the grand homes of past wealthy landowners, set in their lush parklands). Actors, decked out in 'period costume', are often hired to re-enact the lives of those who once lived there. No mention is made of the fact that many of these places were built on the wealth that was made out of the slave trade. In other parts of the world, 'authentic traditional culture' is promoted to give the population a sense of its 'self' that similarly suits the status quo:

> Despite the surface democratic structure, India is ruled by an alliance of capitalists and the feudal lords. One of the most potent weapons to perpetuate themselves in power is to keep the people backward . . . one of the ways they have chosen is to promote the traditional arts in the name of promoting an Indianness to our theatre.
>
> (Safdar Hashmi, Jana Natya Manch, India)

In our own work, as theatre-makers, our engagement with different cultural forms and styles – our own and those of others – has a different purpose. It is certainly not to attempt to replicate something that has developed from a history we have had no part in. Nor is it to reproduce something from another age as a 'consumable product'. It is rather to see what areas of connection there may be, how different styles and forms may interact and fuse with each other, to create something new and unique; how culture (once out of the hands of the politicians, and in the hands of artists) evolves according to the social and historical needs of the times.

Through the creative exchange, you will have begun to build up a picture of the cultural forms and styles that your twin group works in. Some will be familiar, others very unfamiliar.

Try the following to expand your creative interaction with other forms and styles:

1   Deepen your knowledge and understanding by doing some research:

*   Look at the literature, films and other art forms of that culture. How did they evolve? What different ways of thinking about the world do they spring from? Do they have points of connection or resonance with styles and forms in your own culture?

*   Seek out practitioners of aspects of that culture who can help you develop new skills (dance, song and other presentational techniques). If those practitioners are members of your twin group, all the better.

2   Take an aspect of your twin group's form and style and apply it to a sequence or scene of your own play (see Example 48.1).

3   See what happens when the telling of your story is lifted – quite literally – from the form and style you usually work in and reworked in another. This may seem a bit unnatural and awkward at first – or indeed impossible. But remember, whatever you try is an experiment. It may work or it may not work. Embrace it fully and see what happens (see Example 48.1).

4   *Exchange* the results of your activity with your twin.

5   The intention behind the activities is to see how the different forms and styles interact with each other and create new meanings and a performance that is unique to the project (see Example 48.2).

Example 48.1

1   A traditional Nigerian theatre form is storytelling: the circle in the village, and the teller or tellers in the middle.

2   A form of theatre in Bangladesh keeps all the actors onstage through the whole performance.

3   A form of theatre in Pakistan breaks the set narrative with improvised comedy.

4   In Pakistan, one group works by asking the audience to suggest characters and situations. The 'framing event' may be the company's decision – a wedding, for example. The audience is given a free hand in suggesting the moments within it, which the actors then explore through improvisation.

5   A form of theatre in the UK and elsewhere breaks the action by inviting the audience to cross-examine the characters (this is known as 'forum theatre', pioneered by Augusto Boal).

6   A new form of theatre in Malaysia uses hip-hop as a through-style.

7 In Jamaican theatre, the 'carnival parade' is used as a framing device for a whole narrative – the stories emerging from the characters in the parade.

8 Some companies in the UK and elsewhere use multimedia techniques to develop the story – characters appearing in both live and filmed form; characters even interacting with themselves through the use of film.

9 A form of theatre that has recently emerged – in the UK, Europe and the USA particularly – has been the 'monologue play', where the characters do not interact with each other, but speak directly to us in a very self-enclosed way. It has been suggested that this is a form that reflects very directly a major aspect of modern, urban life: the isolated, alienated individual, cut adrift from strong social bonds and established codes of behaviour; people who seem to exist only 'within their own heads'. (Was Hamlet the first modern 'alienated' individual?)

10 Disability-arts companies integrate particular stylistic techniques of communication into their performances: the use of signed-speech; the use of audio-description.

11 'Street theatre' is a form that has been used in a range of ways – often to provoke instant debate about an issue of immediate public concern. During times of revolution or social unrest, it has taken the form of 'agitprop theatre' – literally 'agitational and propagandist'. During the Russian Revolution of the early twentieth century, it was used to disseminate information about the aims of the movement to remove the Tsarist regime. In the 1950s it was given new life in the USA by The San Francisco Mime Troupe, who used the traditional Italian *commedia* form to create street performances that took a critical look at the social and political policies of the state. In India, Jana Natya Manch and many other groups throughout the country perform in the shanty towns (*bastis*) and working-class districts. Often looked down upon by practitioners of 'high culture', the worldwide tradition of radical street performance is evidence that theatre can connect immediately and effectively with the daily lives of people who might not enter a conventional auditorium.

Example 48.2

Black Fish, Pakistan . . . work through improvised comedy. They have a selection of games, which they improvise around. They describe the game to the audience, who make suggestions for characters or situations. For example, a game called 'The world's worst . . .'. The audience make suggestions for what could be the world's worst job, situation, character type etc. Then the members of the comedy troupe improvise around the suggestion.

Through discussion and workshops, we played with the idea of placing their 'improv' within a narrative context (a new way of working for them).

Their partner – Peshkar, UK – had provided characters and a story. So there would be a play within a play: characters and situations played out around a wedding, during which Black Fish would appear as themselves. In this way, the group combined their usual performance techniques with a new way of working.

(Shabina Aslam, *Contacting the World*)

Outcome

- In this experiment with the fusion of forms and styles, you have not attempted to replicate a different culture, but to find the points of interconnection.

- You have – as with many of the other activities – seen how it is possible to place two things, which *do not seem to belong to each other*, into a creatively dynamic juxtaposition with each other. How can a 'naturalistic' play, set in an English kitchen, be transposed into the form of a Jamaican carnival? How can a traditional African storytelling form be fused with hip-hop? How can a technological, multimedia form incorporate Philippine dance form?

- You may have discovered a unique style and form for your play – one that could only have come out of the twinning process you have been engaged with.

Cross-reference

See Chapter 9 and Chapter 10.

Activity 49 Language (or not)

'Theatre language' encompasses the whole range of forms and styles, techniques and technologies that can go into making a new piece of live performance. Theatre is indeed a 'magpie' art form, borrowing and stealing whatever it finds useful for its purposes. Dance, movement, song, spoken words, lighting, environment, space, film, video, sound. Everything is there to be used if it is appropriate to what we want to say to an audience. In recent years, the use of technologies has exploded the notion of what a 'well-made play' is. The use of 'found spaces' has challenged the authority of the darkened auditorium and the lit stage. The literary form of play, where the spoken word is the chief means of getting a story across, has been required to justify its existence.

However, it is likely that you will be using the spoken word in your play, and it is worth considering how it is crucial to the form and style of the play you are making. Many of the activities in this book look at how you are using language, so you will have already begun to consider certain things. It is worth reminding ourselves of some of the key aspects of our language-use:

- The challenge of 'translation' from one culture to another. We cannot assume that the 'meaning' of a word or a phrase in our own language has an exact same replication in that of another.

- You may be using a multiplicity of languages: incorporating the language(s) of your twin with your own.

- A character in a play does not necessarily always speak in the same 'mode'. Our language may shift, depending on the situation we are in.

- The use of 'the colloquial' is a rich source of language-use. The developing street-language of our modern day is as valid as the ways in which Shakespeare drew from the popular language-uses of sixteenth-century England.

- The spoken word in a play requires as much *exact attention* as the other elements that go into making the final performance. With a group-devised play, where there is no single accredited author (which is the model you will probably be using), the attention to 'the word' needs to be as exact as the attention to the design of the set, or the detail of the lighting or sound. You may be creating a piece that is 'word-focussed', with a dense text, or a piece that uses only a minimal number of spoken words. In either case, you should be rigorous in way you develop the text.

Agree with your twin to try some of the following exercises to experiment with language-use:

1   Take a scene you have established as key to your story and *incorporate* as much of your twin's language into it as you can. Avoid making an 'issue' of it – don't try to explain why or how the characters know this language.

2   If your twin uses a particular language-style (a form of poetic dialogue, heightened speech, or choral speaking, for instance), see what happens when you *transpose* your own dialogue-scene into that form.

3   Take a single word or phrase from your own language, with the meanings it has in your own culture. Look at the possible meanings its translation has for another culture. Create a scene in which the *differences of meanings* are explored – misunderstanding, confusion, conflict . . . and resolution (or not).

4   Reduce a scene (possibly one you have already developed with your twin) to the *minimal* use of words needed to express the thoughts and feelings of the characters.

5   Make lists of words – from your own language and that of your twin – whose meaning you are not certain of, but whose *sound* is attractive to you. Create a speech for a character in which those words are central. Decide what emotion or thought the character is attempting to express. Use the sound of the words to help convey the 'meaning'.

6   Take a classical, well-known play and *combine* its language with contemporary language.

7   *Exchange* the results with your twin.

Cross-reference

See Activity 58.

8 Structure

A play has a shape. This might seem obvious: it is an event that takes place over a specific period of time, with a beginning and an end. But in different cultures and at different historical times, the shape of the play in between the beginning and the end has varied enormously. A playwright will tell you that part of his or her task is to give the play its shape and structure – and good actors will instinctively know if a structure is 'not working'. In a group-created piece of new theatre, this task should be just as important: the structure of your play is the great guide for the audience in the journey you are taking them on.

Part of the exchange between twinned groups will be to take on board different and culturally specific 'play shapes' or 'story structures', and to develop new ones that emerge from the collaboration. In this chapter, we will look at:

- what we mean by structure;
- different existing story-structures;
- examples of new story-structures that have been developed during twinning projects.

Activity 50 What is structure?

1   Make a list of what words or phrases come to mind that describe what a story-structure might be. There is no right or wrong here – what you are seeking are helpful ways of expressing what you mean as 'structure'.

2   Exchange lists with your twin group. Have you given each other new ways of thinking about the shape of a story?

Example 50.1

1 Here are some examples of words and phrases that groups in the UK offered as ways of thinking about story-structure:

- the skeleton
- the pattern
- the plan of action
- the architecture of the building.

2 Here are some examples from other cultures (translated here into English):

- the framework
- the course of the river
- the foundations
- the map through the forest.

Activity 51 Existing story structures

Across the world and across time, there are many story- or play-structures that are common to different cultures. A wonderful aspect of worldwide story-telling is these underlying structures that unite different traditions of stories. Even though the story itself may be unfamiliar to us, the structure may familiar and can guide us through this new story-world.

In this activity, use *simple line drawings* to identify and depict story-structures that you are familiar with, or that you are using in the work you are making. The visual aid will help you to be as clear as possible about what you mean by the type of structure.

Send your findings to your twin. When you receive their findings, see if there are structures that are new to you.

See if any of the story-structures offered by your twin can be adopted or adapted by your group in the work you are making.

Example 51.1

Here are some examples of story-structures (in line-drawing form) that twinned groups have shared with each other.

1 Figure 8.1 shows a *linear* narrative. The story goes in a straight line from beginning to end. There may be time-gaps in the sequence of scenes (Act 2 takes place a week after Act 1, for example), but everything progresses in a strictly orderly fashion. Greek tragedies and Shakespeare's plays follow this classic structure.

2 Figure 8.2 shows a *disrupted narrative*. The linear progression is broken up, so that the story goes back and forth in time. Plays use 'flashback'

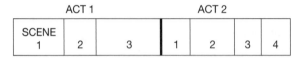

Figure 8.1 A linear play in two acts

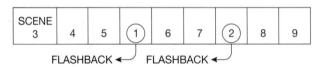

Figure 8.2 A linear play with flashbacks

Figure 8.3 'Chinese box' stories A–D

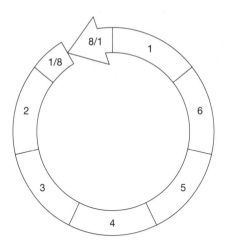

Figure 8.4 A circular story: scenes 1 and 8 are the same

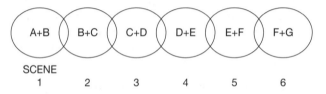

Figure 8.5 Characters A–G in a 'relay-race' story

or 'flash forward' sequences – for example, when a character remembers something about the past that is then depicted dramatically. *The Death of a Salesman* by Arthur Miller uses this structure.

3   Figure 8.3 shows a *Chinese box* or *Russian doll* structure. It is one big, linear story that contains within it a series of other stories that exist in their own right and have no connection with the main story. An example of this type of structure is the ancient Persian tale *One Thousand and One Nights*.

4   Figure 8.4 shows a *circular narrative*. The journey of the play ends up exactly where it began. This can operate as the main body of the play being one long flashback, in which the mysteries of the first scene are finally revealed at the end. In some folk tales it takes the form of an object being passed from hand to hand and ending up in the same hands it started in.

5   Figure 8.5 shows a *relay race narrative*, where one character from each scene passes on into the next scene.

Activity 52 New story structures

Theatre constantly evolves. Old forms, styles and structures may inspire us, but we should not be afraid to challenge them and experiment with the new. In a twinning process – where different cultural traditions meet – there is an ideal opportunity to develop new ways of thinking about how a play is structured. Indeed, it is the 'challenge of the difference' that is once again the great opportunity.

1   Discuss how the collaboration with your twin group has brought new creative ideas into your work (one participant said, 'how the ideas of the other group have infected everything we are doing').

2   Look at how the very structure of your play can reflect the collaboration. How much of the collaboration has 'infected' the actual shape of the story – creating a structure that is entirely new and unique? How far down the path of creating a shared structure can you go? It might be that you elect to create one whole play together, or you might decide that only certain elements of your twin's play informs the structure. Whatever is the course you decide upon, the aim is to allow your play – its final shape – to reflect the collaboration.

3   Make simple line drawings of the shape or shapes of your play and how it is evolving. Share them with your twin. See where the intersections and connections are, and how they can be strengthened and developed.

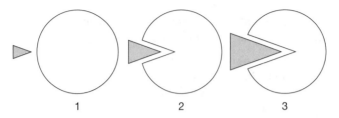

1   2   3

Figure 8.6 An outside event intrudes and disrupts

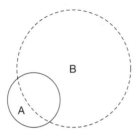

Figure 8.7 A magical world (B)
enhances the real world (A)

Figure 8.8 The past (A) intrudes on the
present (B)

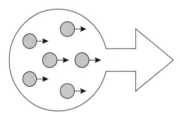

Figure 8.9 Different characters on a similar journey

Figure 8.10 Two stories run parallel, then interact and join

Example 52.1

Here are some examples (in line-drawing form) that show how different twinned groups have evolved play-structures that mirror, intersect with or fully join with each other. In their different ways they all demonstrate how the *narrative dynamic* of a play is not something that 'just happens', but it a carefully constructed artifice.

1   Figures 8.6 and 8.7:
   •   Figure 8.6 shows how a new arrival (an individual or a group) into an established and conventional situation disrupts the status quo.
   •   Figure 8.7 shows how a daily world is magnified and illuminated by its magical reflection in a fantasy or dream world.
2   Figures 8.8 and 8.9:
   •   Figure 8.8 shows how, in a closed community, the past intrudes on the present world, reviving memories that make a new sense of today, and showing new ways forward.
   •   Figure 8.9 shows a group of individuals, linked by shared histories, on a similar journey.
3   Figure 8.10 shows how two parallel stories intersect and become the same story.

Outcome

We have seen that the structure of a play can be put into words – 'the skeleton', 'the map through the forest', 'the foundations' etc. – and also depicted visually. The visual method in particular can help us to see if we have fully realised that skeleton, map or those foundations. Figure 8.10 demonstrates how two 'twinned narratives' can evolve into one single shared story.

9 Adaptation and its opportunities

Beethoven belongs as much to West Indians as he does to Germans, since his music is now part of the human heritage.

(C.L.R. James)

Humanism is sustained by a sense of community . . . there is no such thing as an isolated humanist . . . nothing that goes on in our world has ever been isolated and pure of any outside influence.

(Edward Said: *Orientalism*)

Art does not respect the makers of maps or the artificial lines that are drawn across the globe. It sneaks across borders and is smuggled over frontiers. Echoes of Beethoven can be found in the rhythms of other cultures; Jane Austen turns up in Bollywood; early Afro-American dance forms transform into the tap-dance routines of Fred Astaire; Cinderella's first ancestor was in an ancient Chinese fable. Two groups of young artists in the twentieth century, from two different cultures, create a new form of theatre from the fusion of their work.

The process you have been involved in has, as its heart, the challenge of constantly adapting the work in the light of new inspiration and knowledge gained from your twin group. Aspects of this have been dealt with in previous chapters. You have been adapting your working methods, the forms and styles you are familiar with, the nature of the story you are making, and your approach to the craft of making plays generally. At times the journey may have been difficult or frustrating – collaborations between different views of the world and of art never promise to be easy. The temptation to retreat to the known, the safe and the comfortable is always there. But this is why the work you are engaged in is truly pioneering – you are on a journey where there are no maps, only the one you are making with your twin.

In this you are not alone. Throughout history, art and art forms have constantly adapted. Some examples have been given above. We continue to see this today, in the ways in which artists have taken advantage of the globalised world: particularly in popular music forms, which borrow from each other across cultural divides, creating 'the new' out of the fusion of difference. Visual artists have opened themselves to the influences of other cultural forms. In some cultures, the seemingly fixed classical arts have built into them the principle of constantly adapting. Live theatre has always found ways of reinventing itself by incorporating new forms and ways of expressing itself. The twinning of young artists from different cultures or communities is part of this rich tradition.

So it may be useful to look at some examples of how art has the power to defy the impulse to 'stay with what is safe', and to adapt and change.

> In gamelan, there's no boundary between what's easy and what's difficult. You can play a concert after two hours practice, but you can also work on something for 40 years and still not get it. Each composition is different to the time and place it's played. The function of the music, and the musicians playing it changes each time. There's no right or wrong, only good and bad . . . You can't worry in advance, because nothing exists until it's played. And if we knew how it was going to turn out, there would be no need to play it.
>
> (Rahayu Supanggah)

Gamelan is a form of music found in Java and other countries in the region. It uses bronze percussion instruments with non-western tunings. Unlike most western music, which is linear, with a clear tune as its focus, it has been described as 'more like a garden of sound'. The tradition of gamelan is very much about the creation of music through a democratic and collective process – the skill of it lies in listening and reacting to what is going on around you.

Rahayu Supanggah is one of the most important living gamelan musicians and composers in the world and has collaborated with theatre directors such as Peter Brook, film-makers such as Garin Nugroho and musicians such as the Kronos Quartet. A central tenet of his philosophy and practice is to *adapt* his playing to the context he is working in and the people he is playing with. This adaptive quality means that the playing of the music is accessible to both trained and untrained musicians. A novice can work alongside a master player, and each will find something that is new, unexpected and rewarding. Gamelan has also been incorporated into the work of musicians such as Steve Reich, Britten and Debussy, and heavy post-rock groups. None of this has meant that gamelan music has lost its unique quality or been 'watered down' – indeed its strength has been its ability to adapt.

We have much to learn from, and be inspired by, this approach. In our own work, based upon the creative twinning of young theatre artists from different cultures, we have already taken on board the challenges and opportunities of 'staying open' – of being alive and responsive to 'the new'. Our starting points may be vastly different – perhaps the twinning of a group that works through traditional western (literary) forms, with a group that is skilled in Indian dance forms. The journey is to allow each other's forms to seep into each other, producing a synthesis that is satisfying, unique and new.

This is the way that 'art' has developed throughout history, and how it has resisted all the attempts to appropriate it by ideologies and the powers that be. It crosses boundaries of time, geography, religion, class and culture – always 'in transit', as it were. There are many examples of this adaptive quality of art, and all can inspire us in our own work. Here is just one of them:

> Around seven o'clock every evening in the port of Veracruz on Mexico's Atlantic side, people gather to play, dance and watch 'danzon'. According to local histories, danzon travelled a single route to here from the country dances of 17th Century England. These dances were performed in groups, in circles, squares and lengthwise formations. From England, they were adopted, and adapted, by the French aristocracy (possibly from the servants of the English aristocracy who fled to France during the English Revolution) and became known as the 'contradanse'. The next stage in the journey was to Spain, where it became the 'cantradanza'. The imperial enterprises of France and Spain took the form to territories in and around the Caribbean (Saint Domingue – now called Haiti – and then to Cuba), where it was performed by both the European colonizers and the slave populations. In Cuba in the 1870's, the 'Cuban contradanza' transformed into what is now known as danzon. It was soon popular in Mexico, following the flow of goods and people between these lands. In the 1940's, the mambo and the 'cha-cha-cha' emerged from the danzon. Later, the danzon itself waned in popularity, but was revitalized in the late 1980's. Today it is flourishing and is danced throughout Mexico, mostly by older people who, reluctant to dance the faster rhythms of their youth, enjoy its slow elegance.
>
> (Hettie Malcolmson)

The journey of a dance form that was found in rural England in the seventeenth century to Mexico in the year 2007 is a fascinating one – its adaptations taking in the influences of the English farmers, French aristocrats, colonialists, slaves, migrants, 'cha-cha-cha' enthusiasts and elderly Mexicans. In your own work with your twin group, you will be somewhere on a 'map' of adaptation. The work will be a part of that great, global and never-ending transformation of art forms that brings different cultures into creative collaboration with each other.

That is the journey you are on, and all of the work in this book can serve it. The chapter will offer a range of ideas related to adaptation. Some of them will develop on from ideas presented in other chapters such as Chapter 7 and

Chapter 8. Others will offer thoughts on adapting the work to specific situations and contexts. We will be looking at:

- ways of adapting the work to different age-groups;
- ways of adapting the work to specific 'ability contexts';
- ways of adapting the work to specific 'thematic frames';
- ways of adapting the work to engage with more than one set of twins;
- major stylistic adaptation to a developing play;
- ways of adapting the work in a way that draws upon the cultural legacies of the past;
- ways of adapting the work in the light of significant current events;
- ways of placing your new work on the 'historical map' of your culture;
- ways of adapting the work to different project time-frames: the short-term project, the longer project, the extended project.

Section one – different modes of adaptation

In the following activities we will look at specific and practical modes of adaptation.

Activity 53 Adapting to a specific age-group

The very first twinning project I led was with two groups of upper-primary children. Quite a number of the activities in the book have their root in that project. You may have looked at some of the activities and thought 'these are not appropriate to the age-group or context I am working with'. Before setting an exercise aside as not appropriate to your project, take a little time to see how it can be adjusted appropriately. In my experience there are very few – if any – activities that cannot be adjusted and adapted to any age-group. The method can often be as simple as looking at the language-range you are using and the general life-experience of the group. You may well have made this discovery already. The following activity may give an insight into the relative ease of this type of adaptation:

1 Take an activity from one of the earlier chapters – one that, on the surface, seems appropriate to a type of intellectual approach appropriate to an older age-group.

2 Keeping the frame of the exercise as it is, adapt the method to a much lower age-group (see Example 53.1).

3 Try this method of adaptation with other activities.

4 *Exchange* the results of the activity with your twin group and develop them as appropriate.

Example 53.1

Look at Activity 6 in Chapter 2. This is about asking questions – an activity that might seem appropriate to an older age range. However, I have used this with pupils as young as 7 or 8, and – if it is presented in the right way – it can produce remarkable results. I have always reassured the group of the following:

- You are not being 'tested': there are no 'right' or 'wrong 'questions', only interesting ones.

- You don't need to know the answer to any of the questions – in fact, it is better if you don't.

Some examples of questions asked by this age-group (7–9-year-olds) have included:

1 *Questions about myself that I've never asked before*:
   - Why don't I like school?
   - What am I best at?
   - What will I be when I grow up?
2 *Interesting questions about the place (village, town, city etc.) I live in*:
   - Why is my city called Nottingham?
   - What was here before my village was built?
   - Is this a happy town?
3 *Big questions about the world and living in it*:
   - When will the world end?
   - Who are the happiest people in the world?
   - Is the future dark, or is it full of light?

Outcome

The 'questioning habit' can be encouraged at any age. Educational systems often tend towards the 'giving of right answers', and the use of the questioning activity in a creative framework allows the participants to feel free of 'being right or wrong'. As the basis for follow-up activities in the creating of a play, it provides a rich vein of source material.

The last question in the examples – 'Is the future dark, or is it full of light?' – came from an 8-year-old girl in a school in Nottingham. The two groups involved in the particular twinning project (the one I mentioned in the preface to this book) seized on this question, and it became a focus for much of the work created by the two groups. As an example of the 'wisdom of the child' I have never forgotten it . . . and the powerful way it said something about the whole human condition.

Activity 54 Adapting to specific ability contexts

One of the most progressive developments in live performance in the past few decades has been the opening-out of the creative field to artists who have historically been regarded as 'unsuited' to the world of the performing arts: people who are not sighted, or who have hearing difficulties, who are wheelchair users or who do not have the 'four sound limbs' that actors, dancers and other performers are supposed to have. This opening-out has generally been the result of the pioneering work and sheer determination of people involved in the politics of disability and its cultural aspects. In the UK, GRAEA theatre company has been one of the leaders in creating opportunities for artists with disabilities. The dance company CandoCo has shown that the absence of 'four sound limbs' is not a disqualification for a career as a dancer. Other companies are beginning to regard the inclusion of artists with disabilities as a creative opportunity, as are many youth theatre groups. The work adapts in light of this inclusion of 'the different', and is richer for it.

Your own project or company may include people with different physical abilities – or you may be twinned with a company that has disability arts as the focus of its policies and practices. All of the activities in this book may be adapted to ensure that no-one need be disenfranchised from the creative process.

1   Take an activity from one of the previous chapters – one that (on first encounter) seems to assume the participants have the use of all five senses.

2   Keeping the frame of the exercise as it is, adapt the method to suit participants who do not have the use of all five senses (see Examples 54.1 and 54.2).

3   Try this method of adaptation with other activities, and for people who have other specific physical attributes.

4   *Consult the experts*: Get advice and guidance from people with direct personal experience of disability. (Here is an opportunity for a non-theatre collaboration activity – there will be groups and organisations in your locality that you can go to and learn from).

Example 54.1

1   Look at Activity 2 from Chapter 2: the one that was about filling a box.

2   You are working with people who do not have the use of sight. Make a 'box of sound' that describes your world (add touch, taste and scent as well, but allow the 'sound' element to be used as fully as possible):

   •   a recorded 'soundscape' of a journey through a street – feet on pavements, vehicles, street noises, silences, natural sounds, human voices etc.; the sounds of a street at different times of the day;

- a recorded event – a mealtime, washing up dishes, a shopping expedition, a workshop session, a dance class;
- popular or traditional music or song;
- daily objects you use that have distinctive sounds built into them – sweet wrappings, crisp packets, shells that sound like the sea when held to the ear, pepper mills;
- small musical instruments;
- recordings of 'instructional voices' on public transport, on railway stations etc.

Example 54.2

In Activities 10 and 11, we thought about how 'looking' (at a landscape or a location) could be a first inspiration for a story. There is no reason why someone who does not have the sense of sight could not benefit from the landscape-location activities, given a little thought put into how to adapt the activities.

1   How may a landscape suggest itself through qualities that do not depend on sight? The sounds, both distant and near (trees, birds, stones, water, wind etc.). The temperature (time of day, time of year etc.). The feel and texture of things. The sense of nearness and distance of things.

2   With interior locations, similar qualities can be revealed that might not be so immediately evident when 'sight' comes first. A colleague of mine, who had been born with no sight, described the room we were in, and in doing so he taught us that we had missed out on huge amounts of *detail* about the space: the textures of all the surfaces; the different temperatures in areas of the room; the 'feel' of the space; the quality of the air in the room; the qualities of sound in the room.

Outcome

Adapting any of the activities in the book to the needs of people who do not have all five senses is not about 'accommodating disability'. As both of the examples have shown, the perceptions of someone who is sight- or hearing-impaired may reveal things that might otherwise have been missed out on.

By embracing the huge creative opportunities that artists with (so-called) 'disabilities' bring to the work, our creative process and collaboration can only be enriched.

Activity 55 Adapting to specific thematic frames

It might be that your project is attached to a specific local, national or international event (sporting, cultural or scientific). The focus of the project might then be to widen the area of debate, engagement with, or interest in, the event. With a little thought and ingenuity, many of the activities in the book can be adapted to bring the subject matter of the event into focus.

1 Your project is attached to a major international event.

2 Devise a schedule of activities from the book that suits the time-frame for your project and that of the major event.

3 Look at one of the activities. Adapt it in such a way as to highlight – in the broadest way possible – as many aspects of the framing theme you are working with as possible (see Examples 55.1 and 55.3).

4 Try this method of adaptation with other activities.

5 Create a scene from the results of the activities (see Example 55.2).

6 *Exchange* the results of your work with your twin. How have you approached the task differently? What cultural similarities or differences are there in the notions of 'winning'? How might you use the scene your twin has created in your own work? Are there cultural differences in the ideas of who can engage in sporting activities – are women or people with disabilities allowed equal inclusion in events, for example?

Example 55.1

1 A project is linked to the Olympic Games. The creative exchange between the twinned groups is not simply to celebrate the games (that will be achieved very well by the media, the publicity departments and the politicians!). The task is to raise thought, debate and critical response to the whole subject of the place of sport in our lives.

2 The 'questions' activities are the starting point: Activity 6 in Chapter 2 and Activity 19 in Chapter 3. They are adapted to the nature of the event (the Olympic Games). In this way, they can highlight – in the broadest way possible – aspects related to the framing event.

3 A 'first major question' addresses the nature of the event and what it represents: *'Is it better to lose with good grace than to win with arrogance?'.*

4 Three subsequent questions lead from the first major question:
   - *'Why do I need to win?'*
   - *'What is wrong with losing?'*
   - *'Who deserves to win, who deserves to lose?'*

5 Three more questions lead from each of the subsequent questions, e.g. *'Why do I need to win?'*:
   - *'Why do I want to win?'*
   - *'What will I get if I win?'*
   - *'What does winning feel like?'*

And so on, until there are long lists of questions.

Example 55.2

- A conversation in the locker room before a race.
- The thoughts of the athletes during the race.
- A dialogue between a trainer and an athlete in whom she is trying to instill confidence.

Example 55.3

- The box activities – Activities 2 and 14. The boxes are filled with objects and items that relate to sports – equipment, commercial promotion and advertising, news reports, photographs etc.
- The food activities – Activities 4 and 17. These relate to health issues, which have a direct relevance to the framing event.

Outcome

- Any of the work in the book can be adapted to address a major framing event.
- Such adaptation need not be limiting to the creative process – it can provide a context for not only celebrating the event, but offering a complex and diverse critique of it, from different cultural positions.

Activity 56 Adapting to more than one set of twins

This book has taken as its focus the twinning of two groups. The activities in it have been drawn largely and adapted from *Contacting the World*, a twelve-group (six-twin) project. If your project involves more than one set of twins, activities can be adapted quite easily to a larger network of twins. It is just a question of logistics.

Take any of the activities and adapt them to more than one set of twins.

Example 56.1

This is an adaptation of Activities 1 and 13 in Chapter 2 – the postcard activities. By adapting the logistics of the activities, the range of creative material can be broadened.

1 You have *three* sets of twins: *six* groups in all.
2 You have *six* blank postcards.
3 Using the same list as in the original activity in Chapter 2, put everything you have decided upon onto *one* postcard only.
4 Make *five similar postcards*. You now have *six identical postcards*.
5 Address *five* postcards to the other groups. Send them. Keep *one postcard* for yourself.

6 Each group will now have a similar set of *six* postcards.

7 What differences and similarities are there in all the sets of postcards? What is surprising, mysterious or intriguing?

8 What do the postcards tell you about the range and variety of life and experience in this 'community of six'?

9 What questions do the postcards prompt?

Outcome

Each pair of twinned groups will now have introduced themselves. They will have also introduced themselves to all the other groups. There is now a 'community of six'.

Activity 57 Major adaptations in the work you are creating

We have already looked at form and style in Chapter 7. You have become familiar with integrating into your work the influences and inspirations from another culture. You may have developed your play quite thoroughly by now – characters, story, location, form and style etc.

There is, however, another step you could take, which is agreeing with your twin group to make a big, major adaptation in the work you are making. This could take the form of introducing a *third new element* into the work.

1 Decide with your twin group to adapt your plays to a particular form. It may be:
    • unfamiliar to both groups;
    • familiar to one group only;
    • something you have used at times, but that has not been a central focus in the styles or forms you are working in.

2 With your twin, agree on the following:
    • This is an *experiment*: it may work or it may not.
    • Don't prejudge the results (remember the good advice of the gamelan musicians – 'If we knew how it was going to turn out, there would be no need to play it'.
    • Embrace the experiment fully and see what you might learn from it.

Example 57.1

1 You have decided with your twin group to adapt your plays to *mask-theatre* form.

2 Bring a mask-maker into your process.

3 Develop masks for all the characters in your play.

4   See what can be achieved dramatically through the use of masks.

5   See how much of the play – the story, the words and the interactions between the characters – can be told *through the medium of the masks*.

6   See how far you can push the play towards being a *total mask perform-ance*. How much information (and 'meaning') can be given to the audience by the use of masks, and what could be dispensed with because of this? In particular, do the masks mean that you can pull back on the use of the spoken word?

Example 57.2

See if you can 'shift' your play into other forms – again, pushing as far as you can to telling the story in another way:

•   purely through dance;

•   totally through song;

•   through the use of puppetry.

Outcome

•   You have taken your play – perhaps at a very late stage in its develop-ment – and made a huge and bold adaptation in the way you could present it.

•   You may decide to go down this path fully.

•   You may decide to incorporate certain elements you have learned from the experiment.

•   Whatever you decide, you will have seen that a story that seems 'fully formed' in one style can be 'translated' into another.

Activity 58 Adapting the cultural legacies of the past

One focus for an exchange is to take a major work – a play or a novel – and for the two groups to use this as a focus for their joint creation of a new narrative. It could be a play or a story that is well known to both cultural groups – a play by Shakespeare, for example, or one of the tales from *The Arabian Nights*. (In Brazil recently, when I asked for an example of a folk tale that everyone knew, the group I was working with immediately came up with *Little Red Riding Hood*, which surprised me, since I had assumed this would only be known to Europeans). Whatever is chosen, remember what C.L.R. James said about Beethoven being 'owned' as much by West Indians as Germans.

Such a focus for the work will bring in its own specific activities, but it need not disqualify other activities in the book – they can be adapted to suit the nature of the creative exchange you are engaged in.

1 Decide with your twin to work together from a text that is part of the cultural legacy of the past.

2 Look at some of the activities from Chapter 2 and Chapter 3. See how you can adapt them to reflect both (a) your world and (b) the world of the story (see Example 58.1).

3 Devise some activities that allow the two groups to develop a shared response to the play – its characters, story, style etc. Use or adapt activities in any of the chapters that are useful (see Example 58.2).

4 Look at story-structure in Chapter 8. See what the structure of the original story you are working with is, then see if this gives you any clues as to how you will develop the new work with your twin (see Example 58.3).

5 The stylistic use of language was looked at in Chapter 7. Consider the language of the original story you are working with, and the language of today. How might you and your twin group combine (a) the language from the original text, (b) the language you use today, and (c) the language they use today? (see Example 58.4).

Example 58.1

1 You are working with Shakespeare's play *Romeo and Juliet*.

2 Look at the 'Who are we?' box activity in Chapter 2. Place in it items that reflect both (a) your world and (b) the world of the play:
   - a news report of gang-culture in a modern city;
   - group photographs of different families;
   - recordings of the latest dance music;
   - wedding photographs;
   - a map of your local area, indicating where young people gather, and why;
   - photographs of memorials, graveyards or bundles of flowers placed where young people have died;
   - flyers and adverts for clubs and dance venues;
   - pictures of lethal weapons;
   - an account of an arranged marriage;
   - magazines with pictures of celebrity couples.

Outcome

You have introduced your world to your twin, but through a range of items that have some link to the play you are both looking at.

Example 58.2

In Activity 14, the items in the box were used to create characters, stories and theatrical moments. Adapted for the purpose of developing new ways of retelling *Romeo and Juliet*, they could result in the following:

- dance music, a bundle of flowers, a lethal weapon: all used as essential to a scene where rivalries and jealousy interrupt a moment of joy;
- a mourning-ritual, in which items in the box are used to re-enact the events leading to the death of a young person;
- the journey of a lethal weapon, from hand to hand, until it is used to harm someone.

Example 58.3

1   A creative collaboration between two secondary schools was initiated by the UK company Theatre Centre. The linear structure of *Romeo and Juliet* was discussed. Four major sequences essential to the story were identified:

- the dance scene
- the love scene
- the fight scene
- the death scene.

2   It was decided that each twin would take alternate scenes each, and that the final structure of the new play would be the interlocking of these scenes.

> These scenes happen in chronological order, so it gave our story a nice thread to follow. Everybody knows Shakespeare's *Romeo and Juliet*, but we wanted to create a pair of star-crossed lovers who felt real and relevant to our young writers . . . and the city they live in, London.

> (Tabkir Udin, Tutor, Theatre Centre)

Example 58.4

The language in Shakespeare's *Romeo and Juliet* may often seem strange and unfamiliar to modern ears and eyes. But if we think about how language is evolving today – particularly the 'street-style' forms that young people create – there can also be a similar sense of unfamiliarity. It is useful to remember that Shakespeare was often drawing upon the rich street-language of his times, and to combine his words and phrases with our own can produce something that is bracing and new. Here is an extract from a dialogue between two characters about to have a fight in the street. It was written by a pupil at a school in the UK as part of a 'collaborating with Shakespeare' project.

One:	Do you bite your thumb at us, sir?
Two:	No, an' I ain't bovvered, *sir*!
One:	Do you quarrel, sir?
Two:	Yeh but no but, so jog on bruvver!
One:	Clubs, bills and partisans! Strike! Beat them down!
Two:	You some radical psycho, eh? So listen up, an' make ready for the next cool babe, she's coming my way.

Outcome

The power of language can lie in its vivid use of word imagery as much as its ability to offer a 'reasoned debate'. In drama, this is particularly evident. The intellectual *meaning* may not be immediately evident, but the emotional *intent* may be fully clear. This is so with both Shakespeare and with contemporary uses of language. To fuse the two is to create the new. If we were to add phrases from another language culture into this exercise, another layer would be added. A collaboration between language of Shakespeare (or any other writer from the past) and the street-languages of today can add a new dimension to the creative exchange between two twinned groups.

Activity 59 Adapting the work in the light of current events

It may be that, during the exchange process, something happens in the world that has significance for the lives of all the participants. An event that, in the new information it brings to our shared world, impacts upon all our lives. The attacks on the World Trade Center in New York in 2001 come to mind, as does the tsunami that ravaged parts of coastal Asia in 2006. In my own youth, the first human landing on the moon had a similar impact.

Live performance has the ability to absorb, respond to, and comment on, current events very immediately. A prime example is the 'living newspaper' theatre that appeared in the 1970s. Every day, actors would appear before an audience and respond to the events of the moment, through sketches and improvisation, with the intention of provoking critical debate. In Delhi, when the government imposed steep rises in the price of public transport (thus making life impossible for many low-paid workers), a theatre company immediately took to the streets with agitprop performances attacking the legislation and played a significant role in mobilising popular resistance.

So, if something occurs during your creative process that impacts upon the world – in its political alignments, its cultural perspectives or its view of itself – you may wish (or need) to incorporate this into your work. It may suggest a major rethink about the nature of the story you are developing, or it may invite a creative response that is more 'at a tangent' to the main narrative. Whatever the case, your decision to take the event on board will require a measure of adaptation that you had not expected. But – as we have acknowledged throughout the book – the ability to be responsive and open at all stages of the process is central to the project. The ability to respond to a major event should be seen as another opportunity to take on board the unexpected.

1 Something of concern to all participants in the process has occurred. For the purposes of this activity – since I am unable to predict what it might be – let us imagine that a war has broken out that has major implications for the two groups involved in the project.

2 Think about the following:

- how this may effect the characters in the story you are developing: the immediate lives and relationships of the characters, their feeling and thoughts; their memories etc.
- on a scale of one to ten, how significantly does the event impact upon the lives of the characters and on the structure of the story? Find ways of exploring what the levels of impact might be, and decide what they are for all (or some of) the characters (see Example 59.1);
- if the play is set at an historical time before the event, how might the story in some way have a pre-echo of the event?
- depending on how central to the story the event will be, how much will you have to adapt it to the new information?
- how can you adapt your story in a way that does not destroy what is good about it, but that is appropriate to the new information you wish to incorporate?

3 *Exchange* thoughts and decisions with your twin. What are the different responses to the event within the two groups?

Example 59.1

A useful way of looking at the possibilities of 'impact on characters and story' is to adopt the pictorial story-structure method from Chapter 8. With this example, you have a model with which to test out what levels of impact you might develop.

In Figure 9.1, the impact of a major event is shown rather like the layers of an onion:

- The event is at the heart of the onion: point one on the scale of one to ten. At this point, the event impacts upon the characters in a very immediate way – in the case of the imagined war, they will be caught up in the conflict (fighters, refugees, captives).
- At points two to three, the lives of the characters will be impacted upon in a secondary, but none the less crucial, way (relatives or friends of those caught up in the conflict, politicians attempting to deal with the crisis).

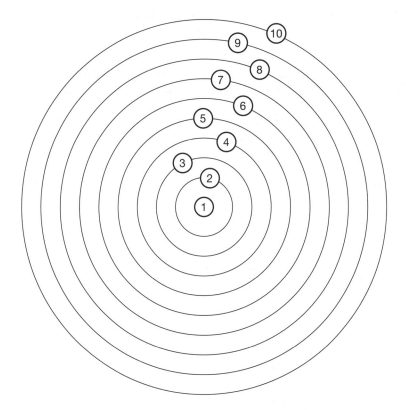

Figure 9.1 A major event (1) impacts on various lives (2–10)

- Points four to six are the lessening degrees of impact on the lives of the characters (a journalist, a TV reporter or a surgeon operating on a wounded person).
- Points seven to eight might involve the revival of memories of one kind or another.
- Points nine to ten might involve consequences for the characters that range from the slightly unexpected to the seemingly trivial (a daily routine interrupted, a commodity unavailable in the shops).

Outcome

Even at a very late stage in the process, you have found ways of responding to this new, 'unexpected' information – an event that demands to be let into the story. The habit of staying as open as possible, which you have developed throughout the process, has enabled you to adapt the work to the most *immediate* of events that have implications for the lives of all the participants.

172 ADAPTATION AND ITS OPPORTUNITIES

Section three – where are you on the historical 'map' of your own culture?

We have already looked at how a cultural form does not exist in a vacuum – it has emerged (like the danzon in Mexico) from a long historical journey, shifting and adapting as it travels along its time-line. The plays you and your twin group are developing have both come out of a similar process. The forms and styles you are both working in have their roots in the past. The creative 'new' that you are making together is part of the future. As artists, you are part of the making of history – building on the past and inventing the future. The following activity may seem like research only, but it may well feed into your understanding of your culture, and how your twin understands it.

Activity 60 Where did it come from?

1   Think about the forms or styles that you are used to working in. They are familiar to you and are part of the cultural world you inhabit. They may be:

- verbal – oral tradition or literary;
- dance-based;
- music-based;
- based on traditional tales or mythologies;
- classical or contemporary;
- social realist or abstract, etc.

2   See if you can trace the history of the form.

- When did it emerge, how did it emerge, what are its roots?
- Did it change and adapt along the way?
- Draw a map of its journey, with significant landmarks.

3   *Exchange* the results with your twin. Compare your 'map' with that of your twin. Do the journeys ever converge over time? Were they always on different paths?

Outcome

You will have:

- learned something of your own collective cultural history;
- learned something of the collective cultural history of your twin;
- seen how 'culture' – both yours and others' – is not a thing 'set in stone', but something that shifts, transforms and adapts constantly.

10 Broadening the horizons

'The play is the thing' has been the theme of this book and the project you are engaged in. All the work has been focussed on creating new theatre from a cross-cultural process. We have already looked at how the work has other dimensions, beyond the immediate task – particularly in opening doors to future life/work possibilities for the participants. In this chapter, we will look at ways in which the project can expand those horizons even further, through:

- personal contact between the twinned groups during the process;
- the sharing of the final work;
- evaluating the project;
- future possibilities.

Section one – ambassadorial visits

A hugely beneficial input to the process can be the inclusion of 'ambassadorial visits' between the groups. The twinned groups will have got to know each other through the creative exchange, but actual physical contact with, and experience of, the different cultures or communities can add another layer of knowledge and understanding.

The nature of the visits will depend on the scope and scale of the project. For two schools or youth groups working in the same area or region, the logistics will be fairly easy. Visits to another part of the country, or to another country, will require more preparation (and bigger budgets!). But the value of such visits is immense, and if you have the time and the resources to arrange them you will find that they enrich the project. It is not part of the function of this book to give advice on funding, but there are sources of grants and bursaries for travel available from a range of organisations or funding bodies:

- local authorities – particularly in the area of cultural and educational twinning;

- regional and national arts associations;
- business sponsorships and charities;
- the British Council.

And there is, of course, always the option of raising money by arranging special fund-raising events locally – an excellent way to widen local interest in, and support for, the pioneering work that is being undertaken.

Activity 61 Visitors and hosts

1 Decide with your twin group when representatives from both groups might make their visits. Ideally, these should be quite early on in the process – once the creative exchange has got into full swing and the groups have begun to acquire a feeling for each other.

2 Decide which members of the group are going to be 'the ambassadors'. The group should self-select, and you will find the best way of doing this. A good starting-point can be for members to elect each other, rather than themselves. Decide what qualities or experience an ambassador might have (see Example 61.1).

3 Decide what the group wants the ambassadors to take with them and bring back. It should be clear that this is not a holiday – it is part of the research that feeds into the whole project, and will feed directly into the process.

4 Decide what activities and opportunities the group can offer as hosts (see Example 61.2).

5 After the visit, the ambassadors should make a full report of their experiences and findings. This will feed back into the creative work (see Example 61.3).

Example 61.1

Here are some examples of things you might consider when deciding who your 'ambassadors' are going to be:

- some knowledge of the culture or language of the twin group to be visited;
- a particular role in the group that an individual has – the stage manager or a member of the 'scripting team' may benefit from one-to-one contact with their equivalent;
- someone who has never travelled at all and would come to the experience with the open eyes of a 'first-time explorer';
- the inclusion of the group leader, teacher or youth worker.

Example 61.2

Here are some examples of activities you could include when you are hosting your guest 'ambassadors':

- hands-on theatre-making workshops;
- a 'mini-performance' created by everyone and shown to an invited audience;
- cultural visits;
- 'home-based' accommodation with group members, friends etc.;
- sharing meal: include foods and recipes from the two communities or cultures.

Example 61.3

The following extracts from some of the ambassadorial visits made during *Contacting the World* processes are given at some length. These were all international visits, with all the scheduling and funding logistics that they entail. However, they give an insight into the value of ambassadorial visits and what they can achieve; similar visits on a more limited scale can have the same sort of impact and feed into the creative work in similar ways.

A visit to Scotland from Rwanda:

Cultural shock I must admit! Lots of things seemed peculiar to me. I was curious to know the kind of lifestyle our twin group live . . . It was nice to read the name of the African hero Nelson Mandela's name written on one of the streets. It was also impressing finding in one of the bookshops the books about the Rwandan story such as *Shake Hands with the Devil* by Romeo Daleri.

Walking around Buchanan Street and eating Greggs on a walk was a very inspiring experience. The rain was on our back but movement did not stop for a minute. Few black faces were noticed however, so I felt more special, not only to my host but also to the entire land.

We went to a Kilt shop and it was amazing to reading my name included Among Scottish clans . . . I tested some of the Scottish cuisine prepared by Debbie, who I called Mom for her warm and homely care towards me while I was in Scotland. My favorite was the porridge of oats for breakfast! She also taught me how to prepare them . . . For the last night we played table tennis and it was lovely all of us having fun while enjoying the game. All these were very essential as far as developing the day-to-day lifestyle of a Scottish character in our Rwandan play.

(Wilson B. Kagabo)

A visit to Rwanda from Scotland:

I am delighted we are staying with families. We will be part of the lives of a Rwandan family. To wake up in a house in which these people lead a life so incredibly different to my own. To view a country not purely as a tourist.

It is difficult to think of Rwanda and not of genocide. I have done some research on this to expand my previously minor knowledge . . . I am going to meet people who have experienced horror one hundred times worse than anything I have had to face in my life. Having recently experienced the death of someone close to me it is impossible to contemplate having to cope with acts of genocide . . . I am keen to learn more, but wary of the sensitivities surrounding the topic.

Are there things that we take for granted that are not acceptable in Rwanda? . . . Finding the balance between maintaining respect without appearing to patronize is something I hope will not be too challenging.

(Ruth Cape)

The two companies elected to create a whole play together – linked by a Scottish grandmother and a Rwandan grandmother.

A visit from South Africa to London:

On the first day we went to see two plays which were at the National Theatre, and I was interested to see how big the theatre is. At the National Museum I saw ancient material, material that that was used in olden days around the world, and I also saw the Rosetta stone which was written in different writing and languages.

London is a very rich country and I must say it is very expensive. It is very big and they are still keeping the ancient kinds of buildings. It's very cold and London is very busy . . . the whole week it would be cold and little bit of rain. And also their form of transport is different from ours. They are using the private cars for taxis, and also buses.

(Simthebile Myiwana)

The London company and the South African company linked their two plays through stories that involved taxi transport in the two countries.

A visit from the UK to India:

In this report I am concentrating on the workshops rather than the social time I spent with the group . . . Phakama work outside, so the group are fast becoming skilled at voice projection . . . No one is late for the workshops. In fact several people arrive early with snacks to share.

In a circle, the group chant and close their eyes . . . then vocal exercises and recitation of Sanskrit verses and Marathi poems.

The group split into two and explore an idea or a theme which they will perform to the group in improvisation. Tonight the theme is call centres and the suicide of farmers in this state of Maharastra. The group work on this presentation for an hour. They begin with an in-depth discussion of the theme they want to present and what they want to communicate to the audience. They only get up to act the piece once or twice before they present. This is a new way of working for me – I am used to getting on my feet immediately. I am surprised to see some quite symbolic and visual work deriving from what seems to me a quite wordy and intellectual working method.

Because both Nine and Phakama are new groups formed for this process, both groups are still finding out who they are, how they work, and what they can do. This is an exciting fact, but it does mean that both groups must be careful not to look inward for too long before feeding back to their twin.

(Company member, Nine, Manchester)

The subject of call centres became a uniting element in the plays from Phakama in India and Nine in Manchester.

Section two – the final sharing

The culmination of the process will be the occasion when the two groups finally meet and share the results of their work. How and where this will happen, and the organisational logistics, will depend on the scope and scale of the particular project. From my own past experiences of twinning projects, the following observations may be useful:

- A venue that is already 'young people friendly' is the ideal place for the event to take place in. Is there an arts centre, a youth centre or a community centre that is genuinely and regularly used to the presence of large groups of young people inhabiting its spaces? After having been involved in a creative process, there can be nothing worse for the participants than to find themselves – at the culminating event – in an environment that does not welcome them. Make sure that the staff team at the venue is sympathetic to the project – and that they feel themselves to be part of the event. If there are professional skilled workers at the venue (lighting technicians, stage managers etc.), they will be collaborating with young people who have begun to acquire those skills. Their engagement with the continuing learning process can be invaluable.
- If one of the twins is 'the host' for the event – at their school, arts centre or community centre – they will have the extra responsibility of providing a warm welcome for the visiting twin. For *Contacting the World*, the culminating event (a week-long festival of groups from around the UK and the world) has taken place at the home of one of the UK groups –

Contact Theatre in Manchester. A system of young volunteer workers – not necessarily involved in the creative exchange itself – facilitated the hosting of the visiting groups. They proved to be essential to the success of the event, and indeed many of them became involved in subsequent twinning projects. If the event is taking place at your own school, then draw the whole school community into the event.

- The presentation of the plays is the focus of the event, but – depending on the time resources you have – build in as many other activities as possible. The sharing of work can extend beyond the presentation of the plays and can deepen the cultural exchange even further.

Activity 62 Arrival and welcoming plays

An excellent way of breaking the ice at the first meeting of the groups is to create very short 'instant' plays – 'arrival and welcoming plays'. To engage in a creative activity at this point not only sidesteps those difficult moments of first encounters with strangers, it also kicks off the final stage of the process with the very thing it has all been about – the making of new performance.

1   *The 'arrival play'.* If the group has made a journey to meet their twin, make an instant play about that journey:
    - Take about 3–5 minutes to devise a short performance piece that tells the story of your journey.
    - Use any of the techniques and methods you have developed over the whole exchange process.

2   *The 'welcoming play'.* If the group is hosting the event at their own venue, make an instant play that welcomes your twin:
    - Take about 3–5 minutes to devise a short performance piece that tells the story of how you have prepared yourselves to welcome your twin.
    - Use any of the techniques and methods you have developed over the whole exchange process.

3   Present the instant plays.

Activity 63 Making the most of it

Here are some additional activities that can take place during the course of the culminating event. An event that takes place over several days can include a greater range of activities, but even one that is for a day only can include some of them. The intent should be to widen the scope of the event as far as your resources can manage – 'make the most of it': the hard work, the meeting of the groups, and the uniqueness of what you have achieved deserve to be celebrated as fully as possible.

1 *A public exhibition*. An exhibition of material that has come out of the process – photographs, film, artwork, objects, text in different languages. Create an installation that can grow throughout the event – words, images and objects that reflect the developing 'feeling' 'of what is taking place, e.g. a 'graffiti' wall of text and images that can be added to throughout the event.

2 *Skills workshops*. An opportunity for the groups to share specific skills they use in their work – forms of dance or movement, improvisational techniques, mask-making, script-writing, song and music etc. If there is the time or the opportunity, such workshops can be opened up to a wider public, or to members of the school who have not been involved in the project. Conducted by the young artists, these are another way of developing leadership skills.

3 *Debates*. An opportunity to create discussion forums around issues and questions that the process has given rise to. Have a suggestion board, on which people can place their ideas for discussion. Encourage participants to decide on who should chair debates and if a 'panel' is appropriate. Older colleagues (teachers, youth workers etc.) may be invited to chair or to be on a panel, but only if the young artists think this appropriate. These need not be hugely formal events: indeed, a certain amount of informality may be even more productive. 'We will be in room 2a at 12.00, and would like to discuss how much control young people are given when making theatre. Come along if you are interested' may attract two people or twenty – the main thing is that the question has been raised independently and has been offered. During the *Contacting the World* festivals, the forums created an invaluable space for the young artists to debate and articulate major questions that the process had given rise to: difficult and challenging questions at times, but always developing the central focus of the project – the creative negotiation of cultural difference (see Example 63.1).

4 *Social time*. The moments in between scheduled activities – when participants can socialise together – are as important as anything else on the agenda for the final event. From young primary children from the different communities or cultures playing together, to older groups mingling in the bar or the café, these moments can generate feelings, thoughts and friendships that cannot be monitored, but that are crucial to the human experience.

5 *A carnival parade*. The culmination of the creative process is a celebration. It should be made known to as wide an audience as possible: the audiences, of course, but if you have the time, opportunity and resources, why not 'take to the streets' and bring the event to the attention of a wider public? Here is an opportunity fully to capitalise on the music, dance and costume traditions the groups have brought together, another opportunity also to bring in other members of the community, school etc. Is there a

local event happening that your carnival parade can be a part of? Are there people in the area who are skilled in making carnival costumes? Is this an opportunity to get local television and radio stations to sit up and take notice? Your project deserves to be heard about!

6   *Volunteers.* Depending on the scope and scale of the project, you may involve volunteers to help with the final event. This is a way not only of involving the wider community – friends, families, colleagues – but also of introducing the work to people who may wish to become involved next time. For the *Contacting the World* festivals in Manchester, the volunteers have always been a key part of the event: not just 'willing hands', but a source of enthusiasm, energy and imagination.

One activity I would suggest you avoid is the immediate 'post-show discussion'. Having been involved in many of these over the years, my experience has been that they are generally a rather negative one for all concerned, and certainly for the actors, who – having just 'given their all' to the audience – wish to celebrate each other and socialise. They certainly don't want to sit down and be cross-examined about their process. For the audience, it can have quite a deadening affect – having to come up with 'interesting questions' without having had time to reflect on the work they have just seen. The worst example I can think of was a moment after a play of mine had been performed in a school. Immediately after it had finished, a teacher jumped up and said to the audience, 'Now what did you think about the play?'. That is an extreme example of course, but I can't imagine an audience that has just watched the Beijing Opera, or a performance of *The Mahabharat* or *Hamlet*, wishing to switch into intellectual-discussion mode so immediately. Allow the play to speak for itself.

If there is the request for some formal sharing of thoughts after the performance, make sure to allow a short interval of time before it happens. Elect members of the team who wish to represent the group in a public discussion. Allow the audience to decide if it wants to stay for the discussion. Otherwise, allow it to happen naturally and informally in the foyer, the café or the bar.

Example 63.1

A good twinning project will have raised many challenging questions along the way. The process will have been an adventure full of creativity, joy and new horizons opening, but also with moments of doubt, anxiety and frustration. By stepping outside our 'comfort zones' and into unknown territory, we encounter thoughts and questions about ourselves and the world that may be disturbing, but that are also necessary – to our development not just as artists and theatre-makers, but also to our development as full human beings.

If you find the opportunity to create forums where the difficult questions can be raised – in a safe and supportive way for all concerned – then I encourage you to do so. We should be celebrating the results of the creative process, but not be afraid to confront the issues it may have given rise to.

During the *Contacting the World* festivals, forums addressing the concerns and questions raised by companies included:

- *Fusion or confusion?* What are the limits of creating new cross-cultural art forms? What are the dangers of just making a confused mix of styles and forms? How do we avoid reducing everything to bland 'common ground'? What are the examples of a dynamic, new form emerging from a genuine fusion of cultures?

- *Young and not so young.* What are the roles of youth and adults in youth-based theatre projects? What is the line between young artists and older practitioners – where does 'guidance and support' become 'control and manipulation'? How does – or can – mutual learning between the young and not so young take place?

- *Whose story is on stage?* If we are developing characters and narratives that are not of our culture, how do we do this in a way that reflects that culture with respect? Are there no-go areas for artists? Where does truthful creative interpretation of, or response to, a different culture cross the line into becoming an untruthful stereotype?

Section three – evaluation

How do we evaluate a project and a process that are fundamentally about the development of the creative impulse, the desire to make art and the transforming nature of imagination and empathy?

The acquisition of particular skills and crafts can be noted. The numbers and types of participants and audiences can be logged. The financial outcomes can be recorded. Difficulties and successes regarding schedules, logistics and resources can be acknowledged. The 'success' of a project can even be evaluated in terms of audience-feedback forms, official reports etc. All sorts of boxes can be ticked. All of these can be useful and necessary in terms of such things as future funding possibilities and advice regarding the initiation and management of future, similar projects.

You will have your own approach to all of the above. What should not be overlooked though, is the evaluation that the participants have of their journey, and what that journey may have to say about their futures. As Julia Turpin (Project Director, *Contacting the World*) said after the final event, 'This is just a beginning'. The evaluation of the participants – the questions they ask of themselves and of the process – is a creative activity in itself: a part of the process that opens the door to new journeys and horizons.

Activity 64 A creative evaluation (1)

At the start of the culminating event, you may have devised the instant 'meeting and greeting plays'. A similar process can be used to enable the groups to evaluate together the results of the work.

1   Work in small teams, composed of equal numbers of people from both groups.
2   Spend 5–10 minutes devising a short performance piece to express the thoughts, feelings and questions about the work that have been shared.
3   Present the results. What different thoughts, feelings and questions have been raised?

Activity 65 A creative evaluation (2)

A similar method can be used to think about possible future work that has been inspired by the final sharing event.

1   Each twin works together as a whole in its own group.
2   Spend about 10–15 minutes devising a short performance piece that suggests a new play the group might create in the future – one that has been inspired by the final sharing event.
3   Present the results. What similarities and differences have been suggested for the future plays?

Activity 66 A creative evaluation (3)

A similar method can be used to imagine the next play the two groups might make together, should the opportunity ever occur.

1   Work in small teams, composed of equal numbers of people from each group.
2   Spend about 10–15 minutes devising a short performance piece that suggests a new play the two groups could make together – one that has been inspired by the final sharing event.
3   Present the results. What different narratives have been suggested?

Activity 67 Post-project evaluation

After the project has formally ended, time should be given for each group to reflect on the whole process. This will give the opportunity to consider what has been achieved, what the problems were, how problems were overcome, and what might be taken on into the immediate future work of the group – or the future lives of the individuals in the group.

Section one – individual evaluation

Get every individual in the group to think about the following questions and answer them in their own way. Add other questions that the group thinks are important.

- What image (a moment, an event) of the project will remain with me for a long time?
- What is the most important thing about making theatre that I have discovered through the project?
- What is one new thing I have learned about myself through the project?
- What is one thing I have learned through the project that will benefit whatever I do in the future?
- What is one thing I have learned about the world through the project?
- What will I remember most about the project in one year's time; in five years' time; in ten years' time?
- What was a difficult moment for me during the project?
- What was a 'breakthrough moment' for me during the project?
- Looking back on the project, what would I do differently next time?
- What was the most helpful activity for me?
- What was the least helpful activity for me?

Section two – group evaluation

1 Get the group to think about the following questions and answer them. Add other questions that the group thinks are important.

   - In what ways has the project changed or developed the way we work as a group?
   - What new skills has the project brought to the group, which we will continue to work with?
   - What was the most difficult part of the project?
   - What was the most enjoyable aspect of the project?
   - What new activities would we suggest for a similar project?
   - What new things have we learned about our community and culture?
   - What new things have we learned about a different community or culture?
   - How much of the creative work of our twin went into our final production? Could we have gone even further in incorporating their ideas?
   - How did the role of adults involved in the process work out?

- What advice would we give to another group embarking on a similar project?

2 As a group, make a large, graphic map of the journey you made and the things encountered on the journey. Where was there a clear road ahead? Where was the mountain to climb? Where was the quicksand you felt you were sinking in? When did you get lost in the forest? What were the best signposts? When were you unsure what direction to take? When did the sun shine? When did the mists come down?

3 *Exchange* the group evaluations and maps with your twins.

Activity 68 Wise words

The evaluation process – in whatever form is appropriate to your group or project – is invaluable in terms of reflecting upon the journey that has been made. We have looked at the importance of 'memory' in some of the activities in the book – and have noted that theatre itself is an act of remembering. Things that have been achieved, struggled with and learned through the process will have an impact on the future work of the group and on the future lives of the individuals in the group.

At the heart of the project has been the process of communicating, through a creative process, with strangers – people who come from communities and cultures different from our own. The negotiation of those differences has resulted in new pieces of theatre that are unique – they could *only* have come out of that process. The process has honoured both the individual voice and the collective voice.

In this final creative activity, the process of communicating with strangers is taken one stage further:

1 Imagine this: A group 'out there' has an enthusiasm for starting up a twinning project of its own. They might read this book and gain inspiration from it, but what would be of real importance to them would be words of encouragement and advice from you.

2 In your own words – as a group or as individuals – send a message of advice to this unknown group. Draw upon everything you have reflected upon in the evaluation process. Make it as personal as possible – you are not writing an official report or a list of recommendations. Think of it as communicating with people as future friends. You might do this in a number of ways:
   - as individual-written letters;
   - as group-written letters;
   - as recorded sound messages;
   - as recorded filmed messages;
   - as a series of postcards or a box of items – which takes you right back to the start of your process!

FUTURE HORIZONS

'This was just a beginning', says Julia Turpin at the end of each *Contacting the World* project. You have conjured up new creative horizons through the exchange process, developed new ways of working and made fresh connections across cultural divides. What avenues could you explore for future developments?

Activity 69 What next?

Depending on the nature of your group or organisation – and the scope and scale of your project – find ways of imagining how the end of the present work can be the start of new journeys. You have already thought about some possibilities, through the evaluation processes. What other avenues for future work can you imagine? 'Think big'. Even if the ideas seem out of reach at the moment, seeds may be planted that may grow and grow.

Example 69.1

Here are some suggestions for future ways of developing the work you have done – add others of your own.

- If the project was schools-based, could there be two local schools twinned with two schools from different communities or cultures? Four schools? Six schools?
- Is there a local theatre or arts centre that would be keen to offer its resources to a future project?
- Seek out organisations that have developed similar projects. Would they be interested in collaborating with you in the future? (See the list of websites for *Contacting the World* companies in Appendix A).
- Is there a large-scale national or international event coming up in the future that would benefit from the input of a twinning project? A sports-based event (the Olympics) or a big cultural event (a 'City of Culture' project). A major conference on an issue of urgency, which could benefit from the inclusion of the creative voices of young artists from different communities or cultures – a conference on climate change, poverty or conflict for example?

COMMENT – ASPECTS OF WORK IN THE CHAPTER

The energy the company members brought back with them from their ambassadorial visit to South Africa showed how massive an effect the experience was for them. It was like they brought South Africa back with them.

(Company member, ACT2, UK)

The best discussions happened in the bar, or during the walk back to the halls of residence, or sitting outside in the quadrangle until the early hours. We had a really good discussion with Phakama [from India] – as a result of a difficult situation when they saw our group's rather careless version of The Ramayana. This turned out to be the most meaningful discussion of the week.

(Jackass Youth Theatre, UK)

When we met our twin, having meals together was important – we were sharing much more than the plays.

(Company member, Contact, UK)

The volunteers on the final part of the project – people who had not been part of the process – were inspiring in the way that they fully joined in and were part of the event.

(Company member, Contact, UK)

We plan to run workshops with young men after the project. In New Zealand, there is a high suicide rate and youth gangs, related to young men who have 'failed'. Men are trying to find their place in the world. The tender pieces in the play [between the men], when performed in New Zealand, made people laugh, but not here [the UK]. There is still the challenge of seeing men together touching.

(Massive, New Zealand)

Appendix A: Companies you may wish to contact

The following companies have all participated in the *Contacting the World* twinning process. Some of the companies will have since disbanded, but a majority of them are still in operation. Many of them have gone on to develop further projects with each other, and have incorporated the *CTW* experience into their work.

Should you wish to be in touch with any of the companies, with a view to exchanging ideas or suggesting collaborations, they can be located on the following website: www.contact-theatre.org.

- 2001–2

  Akshen, Malaysia
  Arts in Action, Trinidad
  Bolton Activ8, Bolton, UK
  Contact Young Actors Company, Manchester, UK
  Kattaikkuttu Sangam, India
  Live Theatre, Newcastle, UK
  National Troupe of Nigeria, Nigeria
  Pandies Theatre, India
  Peshkar, Oldham, UK
  Sherman Youth Theatre, Wales, UK
  Stages Theatre Company, Sri Lanka
  Theatre Royal Stratford East Youth Theatre, London, UK

- 2003–4

  Ancient Theatre Company, Nigeria
  Asian Theatre School, Bradford, UK
  Black Fish Improvisational Comedy Troupe, Pakistan

Brilliant, Manchester, UK
Chicken Shed Youth Theatre, London, UK
Cumbernauld Youth Theatre, Scotland, UK
Performing Arts Centre, Jordan
Peshkar, Oldham, UK
Tarunya, Bangladesh
Theatre Royal Stratford East Youth Theatre, London, UK
The Studio Theatre, Syria
Zao Xin Chang Theatre Troupe, Malaysia

- 2005–6

Act2LDN, London, UK
Art of the Street, Ubomi, South Africa
IFAQ, Hope Street, Liverpool, UK
Jackass, County Durham, UK
Macrobert, Scotland, UK
Mashirika, Rwanda
Massive Company, New Zealand
Nine, Manchester, UK
Novos Novos, Brazil
Project Phakama, India
Sining Kambayoka Ensemble, The Philippines
Young Blood, Leicester, UK

- 2007–8

Aarohan Theatre, Kathmandu, Nepal
Al Harah, Beit Jala, Palestine
Bare Feet, Lusaka, Zambia
Creative Arts Team Youth Theatre, New York, USA
Evam Youth Forum, Mumbai, India
Die Zweifachen, Berlin, Germany
Positive Impact, Liverpool, UK
Project Phakama, London, UK
Space 3, Manchester, UK
The Other Side of the Mirror, Gdansk, Poland
Tiyatro 0.2, Istanbul, Turkey
Trupe Teatro Afro Reggae, Rio de Janeiro, Brazil

Appendix B: *Contacting the World*

Contacting the World in 2004 was one of the greatest experiences that a young artist could have. Meeting people from all around the world, it was the world in one place, with all the love and possible energy it has to give. In one week we all realised that this is what art can be about – bringing people together, creating debate and trying to find solutions.

Yusra Warsama, Volunteer and performer (2004),
Steering group member (2006)

Personnel for *Contacting the World*:

- 2001–2

    Noël Greig: *CTW* Lead Artist
    John McGrath: Contact Theatre Artistic Director
    Julia Turpin: *CTW* Project Director

- 2003–4

    Shabina Aslam: *CTW* Co-Lead Artist
    Yasmin Bukhari: *CTW* Administrator
    Noël Greig: *CTW* Co-Lead Artist
    John McGrath: Contact Theatre Artistic Director
    Julia Turpin: *CTW* Project Director
    Michelle Udogu: *CTW* Street Performance Co-ordinator

- 2005–6

    Noël Greig: *CTW* Artist Mentor
    Karena Johnson: Acting Contact Theatre Artistic Director
    Chrissy Leung: *CTW* Administrator

John McGrath: Contact Theatre Artistic Director
Anisa Saleh: *CTW* Professional Development Co-ordinator
Fabio Santos: *CTW* Artist Facilitator
Diane Thornton: *CTW* Artist Facilitator
Julia Turpin: *CTW* Project Director
Michelle Udogu: *CTW* Street Performance Co-ordinator

- 2007–8

  Ananda Breed: *CTW* Artist Facilitator
  John McGrath: Contact Theatre Artistic Director
  Luna Rahman: *CTW* Administrative Co-ordinator
  Anisa Saleh: *CTW* Professional Development Co-ordinator
  Fabio Santos: *CTW* Artist Mentor
  Diane Thornton: *CTW* Artist Mentor
  Julia Turpin: *CTW* Project Director
  Ally Walsh: *CTW* Artist Facilitator

Filmed record of the culminating Festivals of the work for all years was by Clive Hunte.

Contacting the World would like to acknowledge the invaluable support provided by all Advisory Group contributors since 2002.

Contacting the World's growth and development would not have been possible without funding and support from the following bodies and partners:

Arts Council England
The National Lottery
British Council
Liverpool 08
Youth In Action
Visiting Arts
DCMS
Awards for All
Manchester City Council
The Granada Foundation
Charles Wallace India Trust
The John Thaw Foundation